廣州歷史

陳列圖冊

History of Guangzhou

廣州博物館 編

文物出版社

编委会

目　录
Contents

前　言 PREFACE

　　广州，这个诞生过"五羊衔谷、萃于楚庭"美丽神话传说的地方，在遥远的史前时期就有了人类活动的足迹。众多的新石器时期遗存，证明了六、七千年前广州已是先民繁衍生息的一块宝地。

　　广州自古以来就是中华民族历史长河中的一个亮点，是南越、南汉、南明三个地方王朝国都，是长盛不衰的海上丝绸之路的起点，是古代中国最具特色的港市，创造了辉煌的海洋事业。广州优越的地理位置和人文环境，使其采中原之精粹，纳四海之新风，融会贯通，形成了独特的地域文化，成为岭南的文化中心。

　　中国近代史始于广州，中国人民反抗外来侵略斗争也始于广州。广州得领风气之先，积极进取，为近代中国民族资本的摇篮和维新思想的启蒙之地，是中国民主革命的策源地。深具英勇无畏、百折不挠精神的广州人民又使广州成为名副其实的英雄城市。

　　新中国成立后，广州人民在中国共产党的领导下，奋发图强，在社会主义物质文明和精神文明建设中卓有建树。尤其是20世纪80年代以来，广州成为中国改革开放的前沿地，创造了举世瞩目的业绩。

Guangzhou is a birthplace of beautiful myth and long human civilization. The considerable cultural relics dated from the Neolithic period, have evidenced that this region was the wonderland for the early Chinese people for several millenniums.

Guangzhou was always a sparkling point in history of China. It was the capital for three local dynasties: the Nanyue (B.C.204–B.C.111), Southern Han (A.D.917–971) and Southern Ming (A.D.1644–1664). As one of the starting point of the Maritime Silk Route, it was the most representative harbor in Ancient China. The Guangzhou harbor is opening to the Indian Ocean, the Red Sea and the Pacific Ocean, where the arrived exotic culture is constantly mixed with the Chinese tradition. Its splendid overseas trade, special geographic situation and civil environment, created a unique taste of local culture here.

The modern history of China started in Guangzhou, since the Opium War occurred in 1840 and the Democratic Revolution in 1911. The heroic Guangzhou people during these movements were well respected in China today. The modern Guangzhou city was the harbinger for adapting modern democracy, Western science and national capitalism.

Guangzhou had made a great progress under the governing of the Chinese Communist Party, especially since the 1980s onwards, functioning as the front place in China for economic developing and international trading.

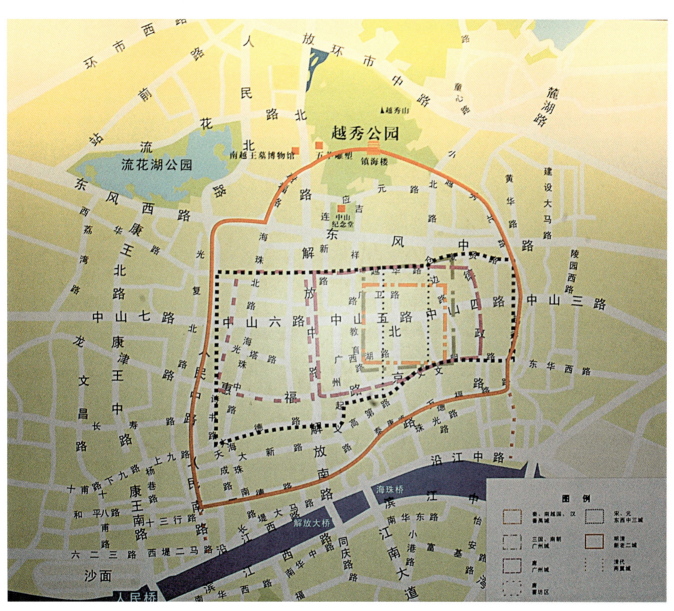

广州古城变迁示意图
Map of the ancient Guangzhou City through ages

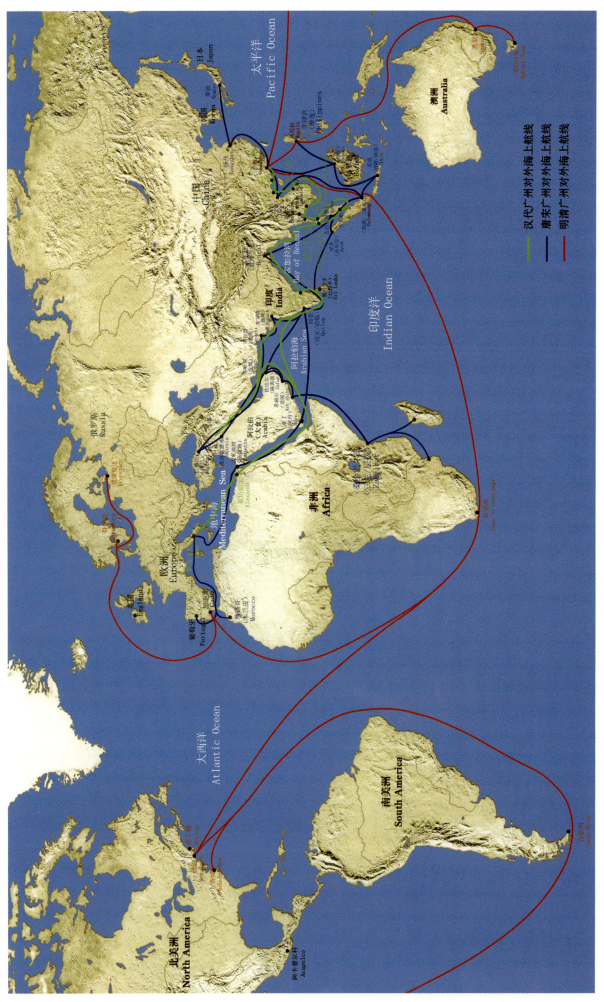

广州历代海上交通航线变迁图
Maritime trade routes in different periods

文明曙光
Dawn of the Southern Yue Civilization

广州，地处祖国南部，位于东、西、北三江汇合处，负山面海。亚热带气候，温暖湿润，四季如春。上古时期，这里草木茂盛，沼泽遍野，河涌纵横，岛丘错落，自然环境优越，十分适合农、林、牧、渔业的发展。考古发现证实，远在六、七千年前，广州已有先民繁衍生息，并创造了灿烂的史前文明。

Situated at the join point of the Eastern, Western and Northern branches of the Pearl River, Guangzhou is facing the South China Sea and surrounded by hills in the north. Its subtropical weather features in warm and humid air like spring all around the year. In pre-history period, this region is full of jungles and pools, rivers and islands, which is suitable to develop agriculture, cattle breeding and fishing. Archaeological discoveries reveal that as early as six or seven thousand years ago, forefathers of the native Yue people had already started significant Neolithic civilization here.

　　相传古代有五位仙人，身着五色彩衣，骑着口含谷穗的五只羊飞临广州，把谷穗赠给广州人，祝愿这里永无饥荒。祝罢，仙人飞天而去，仙羊化为石羊留在广州。这是广州有"羊城"、"穗城"之名的由来。

　　这座铜雕是广州雕塑室尹积昌、孔凡伟、陈本宗三位雕塑家，根据上述神话传说于1959年创作的原稿。现耸立在越秀公园五羊山上的大型五羊石雕就是据此蓝本雕塑而成。

　　It is said that once upon a time there were five fairies riding five goats flew to Guangzhou, brought five bunches of rice ears to local people, blessing them everlasting fertility. The five fairies soon vanished in the sky, while the five heavenly goats turned into stone goats and left in Guangzhou. That is why Guangzhou is also called Goats City, or City of Rice Eeas.

　　This statue is the original piece created by Guangzhou sculptors Yin Jichang, Kong Fanwei, Chen Benzong in 1959. It is inspired by an ancient local myth. The huge stone statue of Five Goats, now stands on the top of the Wuyang Hill in Yuexiu Park, is copied from this piece.

　　增城市金兰寺贝丘遗址，位于增城三江镇金兰寺村，1961年发掘，为新石器时期至战国时期的文化遗址，对研究广东省古文化遗址的早晚关系提供了重要的地层关系。（增城市博物馆提供）

Site of Beiqiu, Jinlansi village, Sanjiang town, Zengcheng city, discovered in 1961, dated from the Neolithic to the Warring States period, providing the important stratigraphic sequence for the chronological studies on the early civilization in Guangdong.(provided by Zeng Museum)

增城市金兰寺贝丘遗址出土的陶片（增城市博物馆提供）
Pottery sherds excavated from the site of Beiqiu, Jinlan Temple, Zengcheng City.(provided by Zeng Museum)

从化市吕田狮象遗址，2002年底发掘，为新石器时代晚期和商周时期的文化遗存，具有粤北石峡文化和珠江三角洲文化等诸文化因素，对研究几个区域史前文化的交流具有重要的意义。（广州市文物考古研究所提供）

Shixiang site, Lutian, Conghua city, situated in between the Pearl River Delta and the Northern Canton mountain region, which mixes the delta culture with the Shixia culture from the north. It was discovered in 2002, dated from the late Neolithic period to Shang and Zhou Dynasties, providing materials for Pre-history cultural exchange reseank. (provided by the Cultural Relics and Archaeological Research Institution of Guangzhou)

陶釜，新石器时代晚期，2002年从化吕田狮象遗址出土。（广州市文物考古研究所提供）

Pottery vase, late Neolithic, from Shixiang site in Lutian in 2002. (provided by the Cultural Relics and Archaeological Research Institution of Guangzhou)

高领圈足罐，新石器时代晚期，2002年从化吕田狮象遗址出土。（广州市文物考古研究所提供）

Pottery vase with high neck and round foot，late Neolithic, from Shixiang site in Lutian in 2002.(provided by the Cultural Relics and Archaeological Research Institution of Guangzhou)

南沙鹿颈村遗址，位于广州番禺南沙鹿颈村，2001年发掘，新石器时代晚期至商代，是广州至今发现堆积最厚、出土器物种类最多、文化内涵最丰富的史前遗址，对研究环珠江口区域考古编年和文化面貌有着非常重要的意义。（广州市文物考古研究所提供）

Site of Lujing Village, Nansha country, situated around the mouth of the Pearl River, excavated in 2001，dated to the Neolithic period to Shang Dynasty. It is the most fruitful pre-history site in Guangzhou region, which yields thick piles, various type of materials, and versatile cultural heritage, thus important for chronicle study of Pearl River mouth region.(provided by the Cultural Relics and Archaeological Research Institution of Guangzhou)

图为根据广州首次发掘完整南沙人骨架复原的塑像。"广州南沙人"，约3～4千年前，经鉴定，"南沙人"属亚美人种，男性，45～50岁，身高1.70米。（广州市文物考古研究所提供）

Reconstruction of Nansha Man based on its complete skeleton first excavated from Guangzhou, dated to 3 or 4 thousand years from today. Anthropological speaking, Nansha Man belongs to Armenian group, male，45～50 years old, Ly1.70 m in height.(provided by the Cultural Relics and Archaeological Research Institution of Guangzhou)

陶器座，商时期，2001年广州南沙鹿颈村遗址出土。（广州市文物考古研究所提供）

Pottery vase with round foot, Shang Dynasty, from Site of Lujing Village, Nanshan, Guangzhou in 2001.(provided by the Cultural Relics and Archaeological Research Institution of Guangzhou)

陶釜，商时期，2001年广州南沙鹿颈村遗址出土。（广州市文物考古研究所提供）

Pottery pot *fu*, Shang Dynasty, from Site of Lujing Village, Nanshan, Guangzhou in 2001.(provided by the Cultural Relics and Archaeological Research Institution of Guangzhou)

双肩石锛，商时期，2001年广州南沙鹿颈村遗址出土。（广州市文物考古研究所提供）

Stone weapon *ben* with two shoulders dated to Shang Dynasty, from Site of Lujing Village, Nanshan, Guangzhou in 2001.(provided by the Cultural Relics and Archaeological Research Institution of Guangzhou)

有段有肩石锛，商时期，2001年广州南沙鹿颈村遗址出土。（广州市文物考古研究所提供）

Stone weapon ben with shoulder and handle, Shang Dynasty, from Site of Lujing Village, Nansha, Guangzhou in 2001.(provided by the Cultural Relics and Archaeological Research Institution of Guangzhou)

石璋，商时期，2001年广州南沙鹿颈村遗址出土。（广州市文物考古研究所提供）

Stone ritual ware *zhang*, Shang Dynasty, from Site of Lujing Village, Nansha, Guangzhou in 2001.(provided by the Cultural Relics and Archaeological Research Institution of Guangzhou)

骨箭镞，商时期，2001年广州南沙鹿颈村遗址出土。（广州市文物考古研究所提供）

Bone arrow head, Shang Dynasty, from Site of Lujing Village, Nansha, Guangzhou in 2001.(provided by the Cultural Relics and Archaeological Research Institution of Guangzhou)

　　飞鹅岭新石器遗址，位于广州市龙洞东南，1957年发掘。遗址包括飞鹅岭、青山岗、菱塘岗等山丘，年代为新石器晚期至春秋时期。经济生活主要是以锄耕农业为主。

　　Feieling Neolithic site is located in southeast of Longdong, Guangzhou, excavated in 1957. Sites include the Feieling, Qingshangang, Lingtanggang, dated to the late Neolithic to the Spring & Autumn period. It was a typical ploughing agriculture.

　　石矛，新石器时期，广州飞鹅岭新石器遗址出土。

　　Stone spear，Neolithic period, from Feieling Neolithic site, Guangzhou.

　　陶豆，新石器时期，广州龙眼洞采集。

　　Pottery food container *dou*, Neolithic period, gathered from Longyandong, Guangzhou.

　　萝岗越人墓是一座以石块筑壁的石椁墓。2004年发掘，墓圹为狭长形浅坑，三壁以石块垒筑，北壁设木质挡板，底部铺小石子。出土30余件越式陶器，有陶瓿、罐，还有盒、碗、杯等青釉原始瓷器。该墓属先秦时期越人墓。（广州市文物考古研究所提供）

Yueren tomb from Luogang is a stone tomb dated to the Pre-Qin period, belong to the local Yue ethnic people, excavated in 2004. The tomb pit is in shallow rectangular, its three side of walls are built in stone slabs and wooden panel for the northern wall, with chamber ground made in pebble stone. More than 30 pieces of blue grazed potteries in Yun style are found, including vases decorated with or check motifs, boxes, bowls, and cups with some carvings. (provided by the Cultural Relics and Archaeological Research Institution of Guangzhou)

　　勾连雷纹陶瓿，春秋，1999年广州萝岗锥林岗遗址出土。（广州市文物考古研究所提供）

Pottery vase with lid decorated with throne motif, Spring & Autumn period, from Zhuilingang, Luogang, Guangzhou,1999. (provided by the Cultural Relics and Archaeological Research Institution of Guangzhou)

　　陶匜，战国末至南越国时期，2004年广州萝岗园岗山出土。（广州市文物考古研究所提供）

Pottery Pitcher *yi*, the end of the Warring States Period to the Nanyue Period, from Yuangangshan, Luogang, Guangzhou, 2004.(provided by the Cultural Relics and Archaeological Research Institution of Guangzhou)

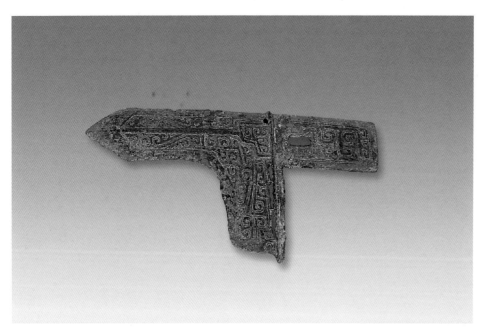

　　铜戈，春秋，1956年萝岗出土。兵器，造型具有南方特色，两面铸有云雷纹，与中原地区所见不同。

Bronze weapon "*ge*", in southern style, casted clouds motif on both sides, Spring & Autumn period, from Luogang, Guangzhou, 1956.

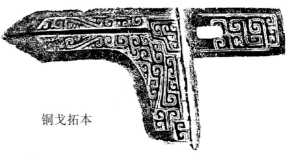

铜戈拓本

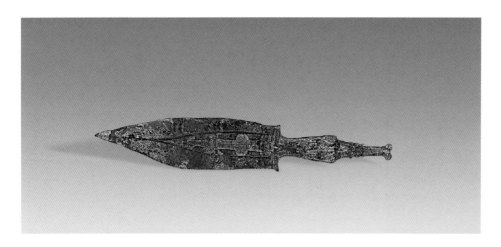

　　铜短剑，春秋，1956年萝岗出土。

　　兵器，造型具有南方特色，与中原地区所见不同。岭南青铜器铸造出现较晚，大致相当于中原地区春秋战国时期。出土器物大多具有南方地方特色，如礼器、工具和杂器等体型较小、体积较薄。

Bronze short sword, in southern style, very different from the ones from Central Plain, Spring & Autumn period, from Luogang, Guangzhou,1956. The bronze culture in Lingnan developed later that the Central Plain, first appeared in Spring & Autumn period. The Southern style features in small and thin ritual wares, tools, and daily wares.

铜短剑拓本

铜编钟，战国，增城石滩出土。
A series of "*bian zhong*" （bronze music instrument）, Warring States Period, excavated from the pebble beach, Zengcheng City.

古代越人风俗表
Customs of Ancient Nanyue People

习　　俗	说　　明
善舟习水 Good at shipping and swimming	古代越人居住环境多江河湖海，故越人熟悉水性，善于用舟。越人多着短袖衣服，跣足不履，便于涉水行舟。
断发文身 Cutting hair up to the shoulder	断发即将头发剪短，文身即在脸上或身上刻刺各种花纹，并涂上颜色。据说，这样可以下水避虫蛇之害，也有先祖崇拜的含义。
干栏巢居 Live in wooden nestle on the tree	干栏建筑是下面用多根柱子作支撑，房子建在柱子上，人栖其上，下养牲畜。岭南地区多雨潮湿，山多瘴疠，毒草虫蛇，古代盛行干栏建筑，以利通风防潮及毒虫蛇蚁。
喜食蛤贝 Love to eat oysters	岭南地区近海多河湖，渔捞经济特别发达，造就了越人喜吃鱼类及蚌、蛤、螺等贝类的饮食习俗，还把蛇、禾虫、鼠类视为美食。
拔牙之俗 Remove front teeth	凿齿是古代南方民族的风俗，越族青年男女出于传统信念将门齿和犬齿人为地拔除，表示成熟或婚俗的标志。
迷信鸡卜 Superstitious, to foretell using chicken borns	商周时期，中原人用龟牛骨来占卜，而岭南越人则用鸡骨来占卜吉凶。
几何纹陶 Pottery decorated with geometric motifs	南越人使用的陶器，表面大多数压印有方格纹、曲尺纹、米字纹、水波纹等，学术界称之为几何印纹陶器。这和北方地区主要使用彩陶和黑陶等有所区别。
倚重铜鼓 Bronze drum played important role in sacrifice	铜鼓是特殊的器物，它是南方民族首领权力和财富的象征，还是被人礼拜的神器，还用于祭祀等等。

南 越 国 都

Capital of the Nanyue Kingdom

秦始皇33年（公元前214年）派兵征服岭南，设南海、桂林、象三郡，南海郡治番禺（今广州市中心）。番禺城的修建是2223年前岭南大地出现的第一座城市。秦末，赵佗击并桂林和象郡，建立南越国，自立为南越武王，定都番禺，王宫位于今广州市中心。从此，汉越人民相互融合，共同开发岭南，促进了当地政治经济文化的发展，揭开了广州历史发展的新篇章。考古出土文物证明，南越国时期，广州经济繁荣，对外贸易发达，都城建设水平高超，文明程度达到了相当高的水平。

In 214 BC Emperor Qin Shihuangdi sent army to conquer Lingnan and ruled over the region in three prefectures: Nanhai, Guilin, Xiang, among which Nanhai is centred in Panyu (modern Guangzhou city proper). Then anicent Panyu was the first seat of the Nanhai prefecture, and became the political, economic, military and cultural hub of Lingnan, dated back to 2223 years. At the end of the Qin dynasty, the local ruler Zhao Tuo established the Nanyue Kingdom based on these three prefectures, made capital in Panyu, and crowned himself as Prince Wu. According to archaeological founds, the palace of the Nanyue Kingdom was located exactly in the city centre of modern Guangzhou. In the Nanyue Kingdom territory migrated Han people from the Central China and native Yue people congregated peacefully, bringing in its wake to economic and cultural development to Lingnan. Archaeological materials demonstrate that the overseas trade was blooming during the Nanyue period; meanwhile the local architect and ship building technique were advanced in China.

南越国疆域图

公元前203年 ~ 公元前111年

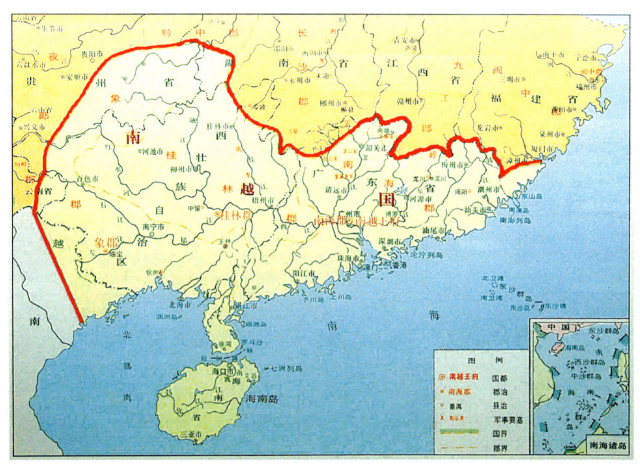

南越国疆域图

Map of Territory of the Nanyue Kingdom (203BC ~ 111BC)

秦统一岭南进军路线图

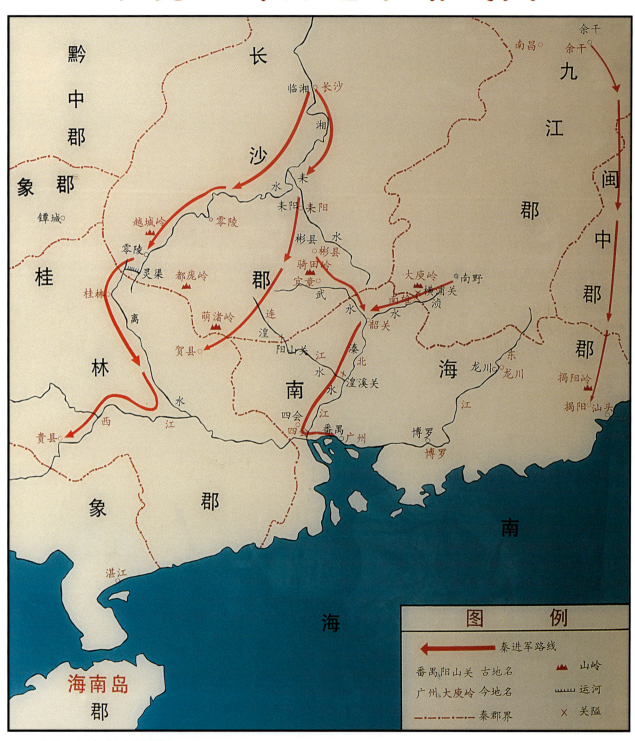

秦统一岭南进军路线图
Map of Conquest of the Qin Army to Lingnan

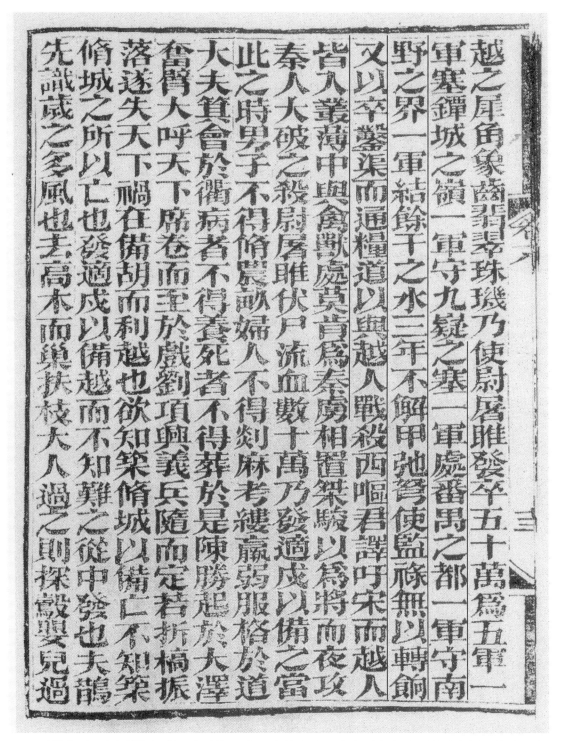

　　《淮南子·人间训》记载，公元前221年，秦始皇灭六国后，派尉（军事长官）屠睢统帅"楼船之士"和犯罪的官吏、亡犯、商人等五十万人，分五路进军岭南，秦始皇33年（前214年）统一岭南。《史记·秦始皇本纪》中有相同记载及33年设置南海郡的记载。

　　According to historic book *Huai Nan Zi, chapter of Ren Jian Xun*, "in 221 BC, Emperor Qin Shihuangdi united six Warring States. Commanded by the emperor, Qin general Tu Sui led shipping soldiers along with exiled officials, prisoners and merchants, 500 thousand in total, approached Lingnan via water road. Among which two branches arrived Guangxi province and three branches arrived Guangdong province. On the way they built Lingqu cannel for transporting." In 214 BC, Qin army conquered Lingnan eventually. According to *Shi Ji, Biography of Emperor Qin Shihuangdi*, "in 214 BC, Qin emperor migrated hundreds of thousands of people from the Central Plain to Lingnan and made it as State of Nanhai".

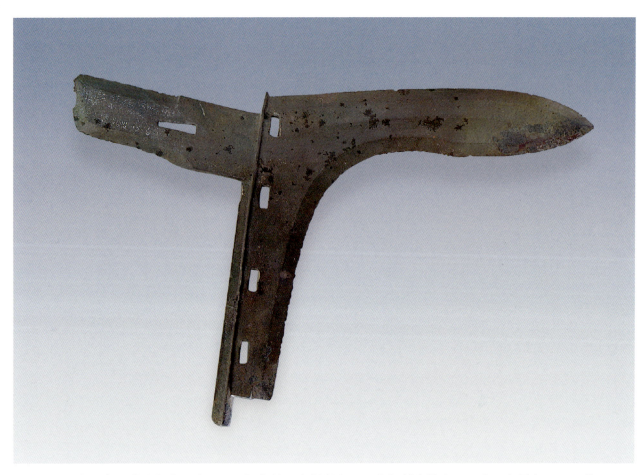

　　"十四年属邦"铭文铜戈，秦，1962年广州区庄螺岗出土。内部刻有铭文："十四年属邦工□□戢丞□□□"，字刻细如发丝。十四年指秦王政十四年（前233年），为秦南征将士所用，是秦统一岭南的重要历史物证。

　　Bronze weapon *ge*, with inscription "the fourteen year (of Qin Dynasty) made in vassal state", dated to 233 BC, Qin Dynasty, from Luogang, Guangzhou in 1962. The inscription was carved finely, which calligraphic style is similar to the *ge* of Lu Buwei, Prime Minister of Qin Dynasty, found in Changsha. It was made 12 years before the conquest of Lingnan by the Qin army, supposedly used by the Qin soldiers. It is regarded as an important evidence for this historic event.

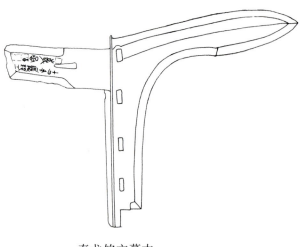

秦戈铭文摹本

　　秦代造船工场遗址，位于广州市中山四路，是目前发现的二千余年前世界最大的造船工场遗址。1975年首次试掘一号船台，已揭露滑板长29米，滑板之间宽1.8米。据计算，可建造宽5～8米、长20～30米、载重20～30吨的木船。2005年又试掘了二、三号船台。图为发掘出土的部分船台结构。

　　The shipyard site of Qin Dynasty , in Zhongshansi Road, Guangzhou city proper. It is the biggest shipyard in the world two thousand years ago. In 1975 the No.1 boating floor was excavated，1.8m in width in the middle, 29 m in length for the unearthed part. Base on this data, it seems the wooden boat can be 5～8m in width, 20～30m in length, which could carry a cargo of 20～30 tons. In 2005 No. 2 and No.3 boating floor were excavated. This picture shows the partially unearthed boating floor structure and manufactory field.

1、方形铁钉，2.4、劈口柴，3、磨刀石。秦，1975年中山四路秦造船工场遗址出土。船体构件及造船用具。

Iron square nail, iron round-headed nail, iron chisels, iron ben, wooden vertical ball, fragmented wooden wedge, grindstone, all from the shipyard site of Qin Dynasty in 1975. These are Parts of a boat body and ship-making facilities.

　　半两钱，秦，1975年中山四路秦造船工场遗址出土。秦始皇统一六国后，铸半两钱发行全国，是我国最早的统一货币。1两为24铢，半两为12铢。

　　Copper coin of *banliang* (half tael, 25grams) denomination, Qin Dynasty, unearthed from the shipyard site of Qin Dynasty in 1975. This type of coin is the earliest national coinage of ancient China issued since 221BC when emperor Qin united China. In Qin currency, coin banliang is equal to 12 zhu.

　　铜箭镞，秦，1975年中山四路秦造船工场遗址出土。

　　Bronze arrow head, Qin Dynasty, from the shipyard site of Qin Dynasty in 1975.

　　鎏金铜牌饰，秦，1954年登峰路出土。

　　Gilt bronze belt plaque, Qin Dynasty, from Dengfeng Road in 1954.

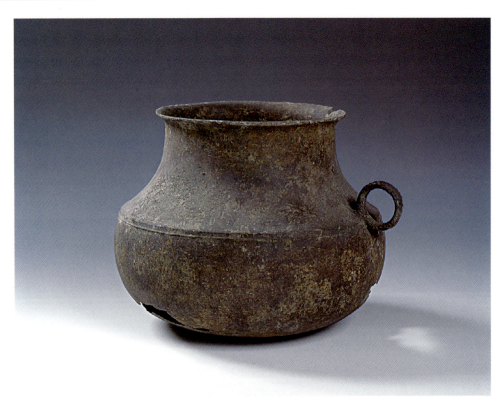

铜鍪，秦，1953年西村石头岗出土。
Bronze helmet，Qin Dynasty，from Shitougang, Xicun in 1953.

陶三足小盒，秦，1962年区庄出土。
Three-feet pottery box，Qing Dynasty，from Ouzhuang in 1962.

赵佗（？～前137年），真定（今河北正定）人，秦时任南海龙川令，汉初兼并桂林、象郡，割据岭南，建立南越国，自立为南越武王。汉高祖时接受南越王封号，称臣纳贡。在他统治期间，能"和集百越"，致力于发展经济，为岭南的开发做出了重大贡献。

Zhao Tuo（？～137BC），was born in Zhending county, Hebei Province，worked as governor of Nanhai State during the Qin dynasty. He united Guilin and Xiang prefectures around 206 BC, established Nanyue Kingdom in Lingnan, crowned himself as King Wu. His kingdom was authorised by the first emperor of Western Han Dynasty, thus Zhao paid tributes to the Han central court. During his reign, various Yue ethnic tribes were gathered together, developing economy and culture of Lingnan greatly.

南 越 国 世 系 表 Royal Family Tree of The Nanyue Kingdom	
一主	赵佗　南越武帝　在位67年 汉高祖四年（前203年）— 建元四年（前137年）
二主	赵眜（胡）　佗孙　南越文帝　在位16年 建元四年（前137年）— 元狩元年（前122年）
三主	赵婴齐　眜子　南越明王　在位约十年 元狩元年（前122年）— 元鼎四年（前113年）
四主	赵兴　婴齐次子　在位约一年　元鼎四年（前113年）
五主	赵建德　婴齐长子　在位约二年 元鼎五年（前112年）— 元鼎六年（前111年）

南越国世系表
Royal Family Tree of the Nanyue Kingdom

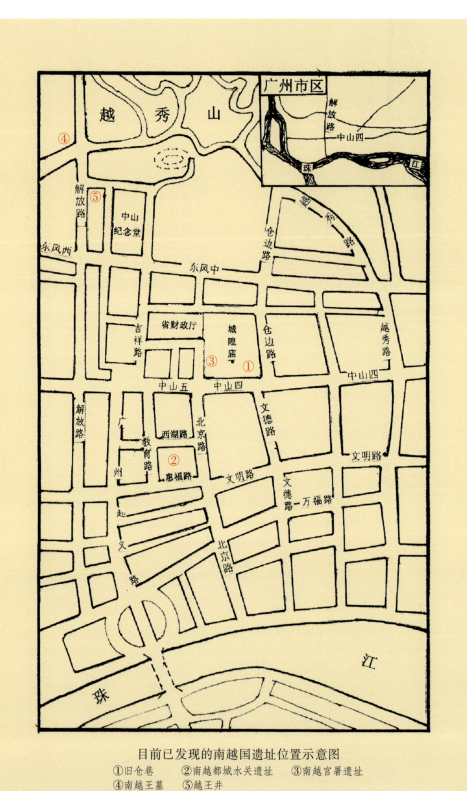

目前已发现的南越国遗址位置示意图
①旧仓巷　②南越都城水关遗址　③南越宫署遗址
④南越王墓　⑤越王井

目前已发现的南越国遗址位置示意图
Map of Capital of the Nanyue Kingdom and surrounding historic sites

　　"蕃禺"漆盒，秦，1953年西村石头岗出土。盒盖正中有"蕃禺"二字，"蕃禺"即番禺，为今广州最早名称。这是秦在广州地区设置郡县的重要历史物证。西汉初年，番禺为南越国都。

　　Lacquer box with inscription of "Panyu", Qin Dynasty, from Shitougang, Xicun in 1953. The inscription "Panyu", appears on the cover, which was the oldest name for Guangzhou recorded in archaeological artifacts so far encountered. It is an important archaeological evidence for Qin Dynasty's governing Guangzhou. In the early years of the Western Han, Panyu was the capital of Nanyue Kingdom.

　　"蕃禺"铜鼎，南越国前期（前219年～前111年），1983年象岗南越王墓出土。鼎盖刻有"蕃禺，少内"；腹近口沿刻有"蕃禺，少内，一斗二升半"铭文。"蕃禺"即番禺，为广州最早名称。"少内"为南越国内史属官，职掌财货。鼎为由少内专用或由蕃禺工官少内制作。（西汉南越王博物馆提供）

　　Bronze pot *ding*, with inscription of "Panyu"，early Nanyue Kingdom（219BC～111BC），excavated from the tomb of the Nanyue King, Xianggang,1983. Inscription of "Panyu" is carved on the lid and pot body. "Panyu" is the earliest name of Guangzhou city. According to the inscription, this bronze pot was made locally for the use of the financial official of the Nanyue kingdom "Shaonei".(provided by Museum of the Nanyue King of the western Han Dynasty)

1997年中山四路考古发掘出土的南越国王宫御苑遗址中的曲流石渠（广州市文物考古研究所提供）

Zigzag stone channel and stone pool at the Royal Park of the Nanyue Kingdom, excavated in No.4 Zhongshan Road in 1997 (provided by the Cultural Relics and Archaeological Research Institution of Guangzhou)

曲流石渠尽头处的石板平桥和步石（由北向南，广州市文物考古研究所提供）
Stepping stones and the slab bridge at the end of the crook (from north to south, provided by the Cultural Relics and Archaeological Research Institution of Guangzhou)

　　南越国王宫御苑遗址石水池中的冰裂纹池壁及刻在石板上的篆文"蕃"字。（广州市文物考古研究所提供）

Ground tiles of the stone pool with ice-crashing motif and stone plank with the inscription of Chinese Character *pan*, at the site of the Royal Park of the Nanyue Kingdom.(provided by the Cultural Relics and Archaeological Research Institution of Guangzhou)

南越国宫署遗址出土的各式"万岁"文字瓦当（广州市文物考古研究所提供）
Eaves tile inscribed "longevity", from the palace ruins of Nanyue Kingdom. (provided by the Cultural Relics and Archaeological Research Institution of Guangzhou)

万岁瓦当拓片

　　"万岁"文字瓦当，西汉，1975年中山四路秦造船工场遗址出土。

Eaves tile inscribed "longevity", Western Han, unearthed from the shipyard site of Qin Dynasty in 1975.

　　"万岁"文字瓦当，西汉，1995年中山四路南越国宫署遗址出土。内为阳文"万岁"二字，已发现有多种不同字体的万岁瓦当，表明有多种印模。（南越王宫博物馆筹建处提供）

Eaves tile, inscribed "longevity", Western Han, unearthed from the palace ruins of Nanyue Kingdom in 1995. At the edge of the tile three stripes are carved, inscribed with "longevity", decorated with dots and rope motifs without grazing. So far different types of eaves tile with mark of "longevity" have been found, carved in various styles of calligraphy, indicating that various types of stamped model of the eaves tiles were available. (provided by the Nanyue Kingdom palace Museum)

印花方砖，南越国时期，1997年中山四路南越国宫署遗址出土。表面模印四叶、菱形纹，四周边沿模印回形纹。（南越王宫博物馆筹建处提供）

Printed square brick, from the palace ruins of Nanyue Kingdom. It is printed four leaves and diamond motif in the middle and "回" motif at the edge.(provided by the Nanyue Kingdom palace Museum)

熊饰空心踏跺，南越国时期，1997年中山四路南越国宫署遗址出土。长方形空心砖，砖的端面模印一熊首及四爪，砖底开一椭圆形孔，以免烧制时膨胀爆裂。（南越王宫博物馆筹建处提供）

Stepping brick with bear motif，dated to Nanyue Period, from the palace ruins of Nanyue Kingdom. The brick is rectangular and hollow in the middle, printed with a bear head and crows. It is designed an oval hole at the bottom in order to avoid the bust during the fining prouss.(provided by the Nanyue Kingdom palace Museum)

　　带筒"万岁"瓦当，南越国时期，1995年中山四路南越国宫署遗址出土。瓦筒边缘饰三道凸弦纹，表面印绳纹，内拍打凸起的小圆点纹，无釉。（南越王宫博物馆筹建处提供）
　　Round eaves tile, with mark of "longevity", dated to Nanyue Period, from the palace ruins of Nanyue Kingdom.(provided by the Nanyue Kingdom palace Museum)

　　云纹瓦当，西汉，1975年中山四路秦造船工场遗址出土。
　　Eaves tile with clouds motif, Western Han, unearthed from the site of Qin Dynasty shipyard in 1975.

　　筒瓦，西汉，1975年中山四路秦造船工场遗址出土。
　　Tube shaped eaves tile, Western Han, unearthed from Zhongshansi Road in 1975.

　　南越国都城木构水关遗址，位于西湖路光明广场，2000年发掘。它是二千多年前广州城市防洪、排水设施，是目前世界上发现年代最早、规模最大、保存最完整的木构水关遗址，为了解汉代广州城区防洪设施、城址布局、结构及城墙位置提供了重要的座标线索和实物资料。（广州市文物考古研究所提供）

　　Wooden Water Pass, Nanyue period, excavated in 2000 at the Light Square, West Lake Road. Dated back to two thousand years ago, it is the earliest, biggest and the best-preserved wooden water pass in the world, situated underneath the city wall, for the city to release used water and avoiding flood. It provides primary material traces for research on the flood protection of Guangzhou city, the city structure, and the location of the city wall in the Han Period. (provided by the Cultural Relics and Archaeological Research Institution of Guangzhou)

南越水关遗址全景（由南向北，广州市文物考古研究所提供）
Full view of the wooden water sluice (provided by the Cultural Relics and Archaeological Research Institution of Guangzhou)

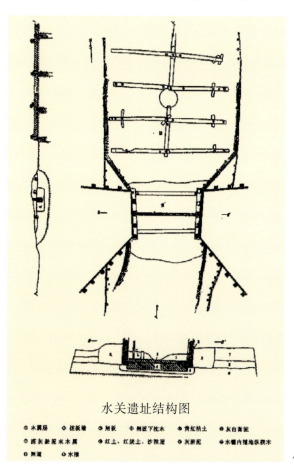

水关遗址结构图

① 木屑层　② 垫板缝　③ 刷板　④ 刷板下枕木　⑤ 黄红粘土　⑥ 灰白黄砂
⑦ 深灰黑泥木木屑　⑧ 红土、红褐土、沙牧屁　⑨ 灰渐泥　⑩ 木槽内随地区敷木
⑪ 刷道　⑫ 水槽

水关遗址结构图（广州市文物考古研究所提供）
The structure of the Water Pass site(provided by the Cultural Relics and
Archaeological Research Institution of Guangzhou)

"常御第六"陶文拓本

　　"常御第六"陶罐，南越国时期，1973年淘金坑出土。罐肩及盖沿分别有"常御"、"第六"戳印4个。汉代少府属官有尚方、御府，是掌管王室服饰、车驾、用具、玩好的机构。"常御"即"尚御"，是南越国少府所属尚方、御府的合称。印方表明陶罐为南越王国少府属官"常御"监造的。

　　Pottery Jar inscribed "Sixth Changyu", Nanyue period, from Taojinkeng in 1973. Four inscriptions are found impressed at the shoulder of the jar and the rim of the cover. The inscription was rarely seen, showing that it was made under the supervision of "Changyu", the office in charge of royal costumes, horses and chariots in the Han Dynasty.

"居室"陶罐，南越国时期，1957年竹园岗出土。肩腹处有"居室"戳记，表明为南越国少府属官居室令所监造。

Pottery Jar inscribed "Jushi", Nanyue period, from Zhuyuangang in 1957. The inscription stamped on its shoulder and tummy, showing that it was commented by the royal architecture official "Jushi".

"长秋居室"陶文拓本

"长秋居室"陶瓮，南越国时期，1973年淘金坑出土。肩部有"长秋居室"四字戳印。"长秋"是汉代皇后居住的宫名，始于西汉景帝中元六年（前144）。少府属官有居室，太初元年（前104）改名保宫。

Pottery Jar with cover, inscribed "Changqiu Jushi", Nanyue period, from Taojinkeng in 1973. Chucks are appliqued on the jar, with the inscription impressed on its shoulder. "Changqiu" was the palace name for the Han Queen, established since 144 BC. Jushi was a royal architecture office, which later changed its name to "palace protector" in 104 BC.

37

越式"食官第一"陶鼎，南越国时期，1953年梓元岗出土。腹部刻篆字"食官第一"。"食官"为王室中掌管膳食的官名，"第一"为编号。

Pottery ritual pot *ding* in Yue style, inscribed "No. 1 Royal Cushion Official", Nanyue period, from Zhiyuangang in 1953. Royal Cushion Official is called "Shi guan" in the palace, in charge of cooking royal banquet.

越式陶鼎，南越国时期，1955年华侨新村玉子岗出土。

Pottery ritual pot *ding* in Yue style, Nanyue period, from Yuzigang, Huaqiaoxincun in 1955.

（左）　　　　　　　　　　　　　　　（右）

　　陶钫，南越国时期，2002年太和岗出土（上图）。左器肩部饰两个对称的铺首衔半环形立耳；右器肩部饰两个对称的横向铺首共衔桥形耳（下图）。（广州市文物考古研究所提供）

　　Pottery square pot *fang*, Nanyue Kingdom period, from Taihegang in 2002.The left one is decorated on its shoulder with two symmetric upright ears, in the shape of joint half-ring doorknocker,while the right one is decorated on its shoulder with two symmetric crossed ears in the shape of joint-bridge doorknockers.(provided by the Cultural Relics and Archaeological Research Institution of Guangzhou)

　　木简，南越国时期，2004年南越国宫署遗址出土。木简多为单行文书。字体多为成熟隶书，少数具篆书风格。内容主要有籍薄和法律文书两种，属南越王宫记事档案。（南越王宫博物馆筹建处提供）

　　Wooden manuscript, from the palace ruins of Nanyue Kingdom in 2004. Its calligraphy normally is mature Han style, with some bronze carving style. It covers population archive and law documents, belonging to the royal library of the Nanyue Kingdom. Before that there was no early manuscripts found in Lingnan region, thus they are precious materials for surveying Nanyue history and early scripts of Lingnan.(provided by the Nanyue Kingdom palace Museum)

铜扁壶，西汉，1974年蟠龙岗出土。器口部作
蒜头形，肩上刻"攀公"两字，可能是墓主名字。
Bronze flat flask, Western Han, with the words "PanGong"
on the shoulder.

铜壶，西汉，1973年太和
岗出土。
Bronze kettle, Western Han, from
Taihegang in 1973.

越式铜鼎，西汉，1954年建设新村出土。
　　Bronze *ding* (tripod cauldron for cooking) in Yue style, Western Han, unearthed from Jianshexincun in 1954.

铜鼎，西汉，1953年石头岗出土。
Bronze ritual pot *ding*, Western Han, from Shitougang, unearthed from West Village in 1953.

岭 南 都 会

Metropolitan of Lingnan

　　秦汉时期，中原人民首次大举南迁，带来先进的生产技术和文化，与土著越人共同开发岭南。牛耕技术与铁器的普遍使用，双季稻、小米、高粱的种植，多种家畜家禽的饲养，蔗糖的提取，酒的酿造，以及荔枝、龙眼等经济作物的培植，反映出番禺农业生产的盛况。制漆、玻璃、纺织、印染、造船、晒盐、制陶和砖瓦等手工行业技术的成熟，表明番禺手工业生产的发达。汉墓中大量陶屋、井、灶等模型的出土，反映了岭南建筑艺术的突出成就，更是当时经济文化发展水平的综合体现。

　　汉武帝时期，中国船队从广州出发，远航至东南亚、南亚诸国通商贸易，东汉时航线更远达波斯湾。是时，番禺中外客商、货品云集。广州汉墓中出土了大量与海外贸易有关的薰香炉、琉璃、犀角、象牙和各种珠饰等物品，以及水上交通工具。这些充分证实了两汉时期的番禺（今广州）已发展成为祖国南方著名都会和对外贸易的重要港市。

　　The period of Qin and Han witnessed the first massive-south-migration of the people from central China. These immigrants, introducing advanced technology and culture to the South, cultivated the Lingnan area together with the local Yue People. A full-developed agriculture in Panyu can be verified by the popularity of ox-drawing ploughing and the iron farm tools, the planting of double-harvest rice, millet and Chinese sorghum, the feeding of the various livestock and poultry, cane sugar distilling, wine brewing and growing of economic plants such as lichi and longan. There was also a well-developed handicraft industry in Panyu, including lacquer and glass making, textile, printing and dyeing, shipbuilding, salt sunning, bricks and tiles making etc. A large quantity of pottery models of houses, wells and stoves found in Han tombs indicates the outstanding achievement of architecture in Lingnan as well as the high development of its economy and culture.

　　During the reign of Emperor Wudi (140BC-87BC) in the Western Han Dynasty, Han fleet led by envoys departed from Guangzhou port to the Southeast Asia and South Asia for overseas trade and diplomatic activities. Panyu was at a time a metropolitan crowded by foreign merchants and products. In the Eastern Han period (25-220AD), Chinese fleet from the South China Sea further approached the Persian Gulf. Han tombs in Guangzhou yielded a large quantity of exotic articles related to overseas trade, including censers, glassware, rhinoceros horns, ivory and bead ornaments, as well as water vehicles. It demonstrates that in the Han time Panyu (present Guangzhou) had already been a primary port on the South China Sea for the Maritime Silk Road.

衡山、〔一〕九江、〔二〕江南、〔三〕豫章、〔四〕長沙〔五〕是南楚也，其俗大類西楚。郢之後徙壽春，〔六〕亦一都會也。而合肥受南北潮，〔七〕皮革、鮑、木輸會也。與閩中、干越雜俗，故南楚好辭，巧說少信。江南卑溼，丈夫早夭。多竹木。豫章出黃金，〔八〕長沙出連、錫，然菫菫〔九〕物之所有，取之不足以更費。〔一〇〕九疑、〔二一〕蒼梧以南至儋耳者，〔二二〕與江南大同俗，而楊越多焉。番禺〔二三〕亦其一都會也，珠璣、犀、瑇瑁、果、布之湊。〔二四〕

《史记·货殖列传》记载番禺（今广州）是秦汉时期全国著名都会。

Coincidentally, historic sources such as *Shi Ji* and *Han Shu* record Panyu as a famous mercantile metropolitan in the Qin and Han period.

东汉城墙遗址，1996年中山五路发掘。（广州市文物考古研究所提供）
City wall ruins, Western Han, excavated from Zhongshan Wu Road in 1996. (provided by the Cultural Relics and Archaeological Research Institution of Guangzhou)

陶牛，西汉，1955年河南大元岗出土。牛是广州当时社会主要生产工具。
Pottery bull, Western Han, from Dayuangang, Southern River Bank in 1955. Bull was the major animal for plough agriculture in Guangzhou during the Han Dynasty.

陶牛圈，东汉，1984年沙河顶出土。分前后院，内有一人五牛。汉代，广州农业生产已普遍使用牛耕。

Pottery cowshed, Western Han, from Shaheding site in 1984. It is divided into two yards, front and behind, depicted with one person and five bulls.

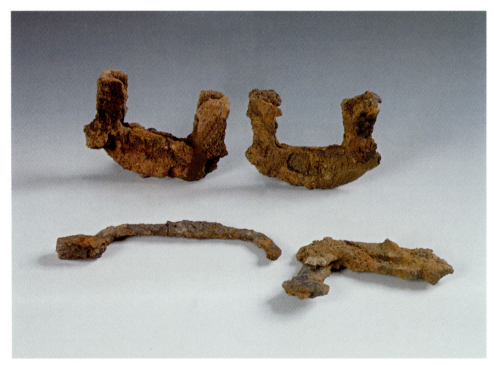

铁锄，西汉，1955年建设新村乌龙岗出土。这是广州当时社会主要生产工具。

铁镰，西汉，1955年蛇头岗出土。

Iron hoe, Western Han, excavated from Wulonggang in 1955. It was a major agricultural utensil in the Han period Guangzhou.

Iron sickle, Western Han, discovered from Shetougang in 1955.

陶水田，东汉，1962年广东佛山澜石出土。这件模型反映了当时珠江三角洲双夏农忙的情景：刚收割完的稻田已翻土耕作，两具铁犁搁在一边，大家忙于播种、修理农具。

Pottery paddy field, Eastern Han, from Lanshi, Foshan, in 1962. It depicts the busy scenes of summer in Pearl River Delta. As soon as the matured rice was gathered from the field, the field has been ploughed once more for the new turn of plants, two iron ploughs are put alongside, while farmers are busy spreading seeds and repairing tools.

陶牛、陶羊 、陶鸡 、陶鸭 、陶鹅 、陶猪，东汉，广州出土。
Pottery figurines of domestic animals, including lamb, cattle, chicken, duck, goose, pig, Eastern Han, from Huanghuagang in 1997.

陶提筒，东汉，1953年龙生岗出土。盖内有墨写隶书"藏酒十石令兴寿至三百岁"。提筒为盛酒的器皿，出土时器内尚存半筒已炭化的高粱。

Pottery handle wine bottle in coloured glaze, Eastern Han, from Longshenggang in 1953. On the lid it inscribed by "Storing wine for 10 *dan* will gain 300 years longevity." The bottle is originally for containing wine, and during the excavation half bottle of durra was found. However, over 2000 years, the durra has gone carbonized.

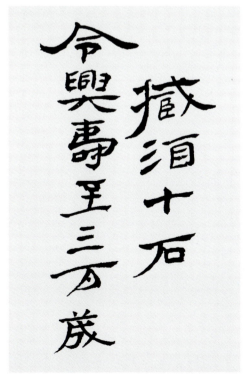

墨书"藏酒十石令兴寿至三百岁"摹本。
Rubbing of the inscription found on the wine bottle: "Storing wine for 10 *dan* will gain 300 years longevity."

陶簋，西汉，1955年大元岗出土。陶簋在广州西汉后期开始通行，常与温酒樽、壶、盒等同置，为盛酒食器。今粤语中仍通用，有"九大簋"之说，意为设宴盛情款待客人。

Glazed pottery plate called "gui", Western Han, recovered from Dayuangang in 1955. According to archaeological finds, this type of pottery plate "gui" was popular in the late Western Han in Guangzhou, normally put along with the wine warming set, wine flask, food container, as a series of tableware. In modern Canton dialect, "nine big gui" means a big banquet for welcoming guests.

　　陶舂米（上图）、簸米俑（下图），东汉，1956年景泰坑出土。一人持杆对臼而舂，一人扬箕以簸。这是汉代岭南地区常见的一种粮食加工方法。
　　Pottery servant figurines pounding rice and winnowing rice, Eastern Han，excavated from Jingtaikeng in 1956. One figurine holds a stick to pound the rice in a mortar, and one is winnowing to seperate the chaff. This is the common method for making eatable rice used in Lingnan during the Han period.

陶仓，东汉，1956年龙生岗出土。贮存粮食的干栏式建筑模型，长方形。面宽三间，前部为横廊，后部为仓室。门前设板梯，以供上下。仓房高架于四根陶质圆柱上，以利通风防潮。这是适应南方多雨潮湿的天气。

Pottery granary, Eastern Han, from Longshenggang in 1956. Shaped in rectangular for containing crops, built with barriers. It is divided into three rooms, a horizontal corrdor in front and a granary behind. Staircase is made in front of the gate. The granary is built highly on four round pottery pillars, in order to have fresh air and avovd moisturs. This design suits the rainy and humid weather in the south.

陶囷，东汉，1954年东山出土。囷盖如伞形，遍刻下垂的蓖状纹，显示是用稻秆编织、分层叠盖的。囷体圆形，除门洞外，密封防潮；围壁划有似竹木结构的线纹，开长方形门口，旁边刻划门框的线条，两侧各有二穿孔，是栓门扇之用。囷是贮存粮食的干栏式建筑。

Two-storey pottery granary, Eastern Han, from Dongshan, in 1954. The granary roof looks like a canopy carved with drifting lines, showing that the roof is covered by straw stern in a couple of levels. The granary is shaped in cylinder, and well sealed excepted for a door hole, in order to avoid the dump air. The wall is covered over by bamboo sterns. The door is in rectangular, two holes are made in both sides for door bar. This type of granary in two storey is ideal for storing grains under warm and humid weather.

盛放在陶五联罐内的酸梅
The sow palm contained in five jointed pottery jars

盛放在陶四耳罐内的橄榄
The canary fruit (Canarium album) contained in pottery jar with four lugs

　　漆套盒，东汉，1953年龙生岗出土。器分盖、身、底三节。套合成上、下两成。夹绫胎，髹漆光亮，制作精工。

　　A series of lacquer boxes, Eastern Han, excavated from Longshenggang in 1953. Each piece has a cover, body and foot. It was put one by one from the small to the large. The lacquers are in shining glaze and delicately made.

　　"永元十六年三月作东冶桥北陈次华灶"铭文墓砖，东汉，1972年克山出土。永元十六年即104年，陈次华灶指"陈次华窑"，是东汉私人开设的砖窑。

　　Tomb brick with inscription, dated to 104AD, Eastern Han, from Keshan in 1972. It is inscribed "March of the sixteenth year of Yongyuan era, made in private kiln of Chen Cihua north of the Dongye Bridge". It is worth noting that, according to the inscription, as early as Han time the private kiln was set up in Guangzhou.

　　海幢寺汉代窑址，位于广州同福中路，1996年7月进行发掘。出土陶器种类丰富，主要有瓮、罐、碗等。陶质以夹细砂的红陶、灰陶、釉陶为主，纹饰以方格印纹、方格印纹加戳印纹为主等等。窑址的发掘，表明今海幢公园一带是广州重要的汉代窑场分布区。（广州市文物考古研究所提供）

Han kiln site in Haichuang Temple, at Tongfuzhong Road, Guangzhou, excavated in July 1996. Recovered potteries include wine pot, jar, bowl so forth. The potteries are mainly made of terracotta red clay , gray clay, and glazed pottery, decorated with stamped chucks and impressed design etc. It reveals that the zone of Haichuang Park today was an important Han kiln in ancient Guangzhou. (provided by the Cultural Relics and Archaeological Research Institution of Guangzhou)

陶杯、盘，东汉，1956年羊山出土。杯亦称"卮"，原是饮酒器。广州汉墓中经常是一杯一盆叠合成套放在棺具的前端，为墓中设奠的饮食器。杯盆上粘附的聚釉说明，广州汉陶是入窑露烧的。

Glazed pottery cup and plate, Eastern Han, from Yangshan in 1956. The type of wine cup is called "zhi". From Han tombs in Guangzhou, very often a wine cup and a plate were discovered in front of the coffin, as if arranged for the soul's eating and drinking during the funerary ceremony, The intensive glaze found sticking on the cup and the plate, shows that the Han pottery in Guangzhou was fired opening to the air in the kiln.

陶双联罐，西汉，1957年华侨新村出土。有两个盖钮，其一为梅花鹿（鹿头原缺）。以动物形象作钮饰或器耳，是广州汉代器皿附饰的一大特点。

Two jointed jars, glazed pottery, Western Han, excavated from Huaqiaoxincun in 1957. It has two nodes on each covers, one is in the form of the deer (with the deer head missing when discovered). Vessels of Guangzhou in the Han period is distinguished by the use of animal shaped nodes or lugs.

陶三联罐，西汉，1957年北郊瑶台出土。盛调味品或干果的器物。

Three jointed pottery jars, Western Han, excavated from Jade Terrace, north vicinity of Guangzhou in 1957, for containing spices and dried fruits.

陶四联罐，西汉，1955年华侨新村出土。盛调味品或干果的器物。

Four jointed pottery jars, Western Han, excavated from Huaqiaoxincun in 1955, for containing spices and dried fruits.

陶五联罐，西汉，1955年大元岗出土。在四个联罐中间，加上一个小罐。每罐有盖，盖钮为鸟形，平底无足。西汉时期的陶联罐以五联罐最为普遍，这类联罐是盛调味品或干果品的器具。广州西村五联罐出土时尚存梅核，足以证明其用途。

Five jointed pottery jars, Western Han, unearthed from Dayuangang in 1956. Each jar has a cover in the form of a bird, and no foot. Five jointed jars for containing spices and dry fruits were highly appreciated in the Western Han Dynasty, especially as their and feet vanished. in late years Another similar item was found from West Village in Guangzhou, which contained some palm seeds as just discovered.

陶八联罐，西汉，1956年麻鹰岗出土。由八个圆盒组成，其中六个大盒分列两行，两个小合在中间，与大盒相联，但各不互通。八盒下面为长方形座，每面镂空六个圆孔。

Eight jointed pottery jars, Western Han, unearthed from Mayinggang in 1956. Six round jars are in two lines with two small round jars in the middle, but all independent. At the bottom there is a rectangular base, with six holes incised on each side.

彩绘陶钫，西汉，1955年华侨新村出土。
Color painted pottery kettle, Western Han, excavated from Huaqiaoxincun in 1955.

陶温壶，西汉，1955年华侨新村出土。做工精细，黄褐色釉保存完好，反映出汉代广州的陶艺水平。温壶是一种注入温水取暖的器具，相当于现在的"汤婆子"。两汉墓葬中均有发现，数量不多。

Glazed pottery bottle, Western Han, recovered from Huaqiaoxincun in 1955. The yellowish glaze is so far well preserved. This type of bottle is for containing warm water and warming up one's body in winter. A few samples can be found in Western and Eastern Han tombs in Guangzhou.

陶匏壶，西汉，1955年大元岗出土。日常生活中，匏瓜常被用作盛酒或水的容器。仿匏瓜而制作的匏壶是广州汉墓中常见的器皿。这件匏壶上节修长，带凤鸟形塞，造型精巧别致，釉色晶滢，反映出西汉后期陶艺水平的发展与提高。

Pottery wine flask, Western Han, excavated from Dayuangang in 1955. Shaped in gourd, the flask was the popular daily ware found from Han tombs in Guanghzou. This item has a high neck and a phoenix headed lid, with lustrous glaze, showing the exquisite pottery art in the Late Western Han time.

陶壶，东汉，1973年马湟水岗出土。汉代称这类壶为"钟"，是盛酒浆或粮食的器具。壶型体大，造型稳重，制作精工，胎釉紧密，为广州西汉青釉硬陶的代表。

Celadon pottery bottle, Eastern Han, unearthed from Mahuangshuigang in 1973. This type of big and heavy pottery bottle is called "zhong" in Han Dynasty, normally for containing wine or rice. Its fine clay body and lustrous glaze shows the superior pottery making technique in Guangzhou in the Han period.

陶釜，东汉，1956年羊山横路出土。三足釜是一种温酒器。形似盉而无流，用时以勺取酒。

Three-feet pottery wine-warming pot, Eastern Han, excavated from the Yangshanheng Road in 1956. It looks like wine container but without spout, so spoon is used to gain wine during the meal.

陶壶，东汉，1955年先烈路出土。
Pottery bottle, Eastern Han, unearthed from Xianlie Road in 1955.

陶瓿，西汉，1955年华侨新村玉子岗出土。
Pottery *bu* (small jar), Western Han, unearthed from Yuzigang, Huaqiaoxincun in 1955.

陶盒，东汉，1954年羊山横路出土。
Pottery box, Eastern Han, unearthed from Yangshanheng Road in 1954.

陶鼎，西汉，2000年恒福路银行疗养院出土。（广州市文物考古研究所提供）

Pottery *ding* (tripod cauldron for cooking), Western Han, unearthed from the Bank Sanatorium, Hengfu Road in 2000. (provided by the Cultural Relics and Archaeological Research Institution of Guangzhou)

陶鼎，东汉，1956年麻鹰岗出土。

Pottery ding (ritual pot), unearthed from Mayinggang in 1956.

　　陶枭形盒，东汉，2004年广州大学城青岗出土。整体仿猫头鹰
（枭）造型，下接三乳丁小足。腹部有对应的两个翅膀，一边另有
一尾羽。（广州市文物考古研究所提供）
　　Pottery box shaped in owl with three feet, Eastern Han, from
Qinggang, Guangzhou Higher Education Mega Center in 2004. Two wings are depicted
on the tummy, with a tail in one side.(provided by the Cultural Relics and
Archaeological Research Institution of Guangzhou)

　　陶龟把三足器，西汉，2004年永福路广州警备区干休所工地出
土。器的造型别致，状如行灯。（广州市文物考古研究所提供）
　　Pottery item with a handle in form of turtle and three feet, Western Han, from
field of Police Inn at Yongfu Road, Guangzhou, excavated in 2004. It has a unique
shape, like a movable lamp. (provided by the Cultural Relics and Archaeological
Research Institution of Guangzhou)

陶井，东汉，1954建设新村出土。
Pottery well, Eastern Han, excavated from Jianshexincun in 1954.

　陶井，东汉后期，1957年沙河出土。井栏方形，井口为井形的木架，地台宽阔。井亭是在井栏的四角上立四根圆柱，其上复以四坡式顶立一凤鸟的亭盖，以保护食水清洁。

Pottery well, Late Eastern Han, excavated from Shahe in 1957. The well barrier is shaped in square, the well rim is made of wood shaped in "井", with wide floor. The well pavilion is based on the four round pillars at the barrier corners, covered up with a pavilion roof with a phoenix atop. The well pavilion was built in order to keep the drinking water clean through years.

　　陶灶，东汉后期，1956年海珠区大元岗出土。灶身长方形，上置二釜一锅。灶后有龙首形烟突，灶门拱形，地台左侧有一俑，执扇扇水，右侧一狗蹲坐。灶身两壁间各附三口水缸，利用灶堂热力温水。此灶形制设计合理，是汉代岭南人对热能的认识与充分利用的最好例证。

Pottery cooking stove ，Eastern Han，unearthed from Dayuangang, Haizhu District in 1956. The cooking stove is shaped in rectangular, on which two pot and one pan can be put. Behind the stove there is a dragon headed chimney. The stove door is arch shaped. At the left side on the ground a servant figurine holds a fan to fan the fire, while a figurine dog sits aside. Three water vats are designed alongside the two walls near the stove, thus the heat from the stove will heat up the water. The stove is scientifically designed, showing the Lingnan people in the Han period had advanced knowledge of heat and used it efficiently.

玉璧，西汉，1973年淘金坑出土。
Jade round piece bi, Western Han, from Gold Washing Pit in 1973.

玉带钩，西汉，1953年西村出土。
Jade belt buckle, Western Han, from west village in 1953.

玉龙虎佩，西汉，1956年物资厅出土。
Jade ornament shaped in dragon and tiger, Western Han, from Wuzhiting in 1956.

玉剑璲、玉剑格、玉剑珌，西汉，1956年麻鹰岗出土。
Jade sword component, Western Han, from Mayinggang in 1956.

铜提梁壶，东汉，1954年沙河顶出土。
Bronze loop-handled wine flask, Eastern Han, from Shaheding in 1954.

　　铜案、耳杯（七件一套）。东汉后期，1960年沙河顶出土。汉人席地而坐，案就等于现代的桌子。出土时三铜案排列在棺室的前端，正中为长方形案，两圆案分置于两侧。案上还放有耳杯、铜箸等食具，保持原来棺前致奠的陈设。
　　Bronze flanged cups with tray. Late E. Han, Excavated in 1960 at Shaheding. This circular tray was used as a table as the Han people normally sat on the floor. During the excavation a total of three bronze trays were discovered. They were arranged in a row in front of the coffin chamber. The middle one was rectangular while the two others were circular and bronze flanged cups and chopsticks were found on the top of these trays showing the original setting for offering at the burial.

铜温酒樽，东汉后期，1960年沙河顶出土。此器盖顶作重山形，饰以孔雀钮。全器镂刻精细的鸟兽纹，线纹流畅，纹样生动；器盖与身镶嵌圆形或方形的金属薄片。是一件精致的艺术品。

Bronze wine warmer Late Eastern. Han, Excavated in 1960 at Shaheding. The cover is in the shape of stack mountains and topped by a peacock shaped knob. The decoration consists of finely chased of birds and animals with small circular or square metal inlays.

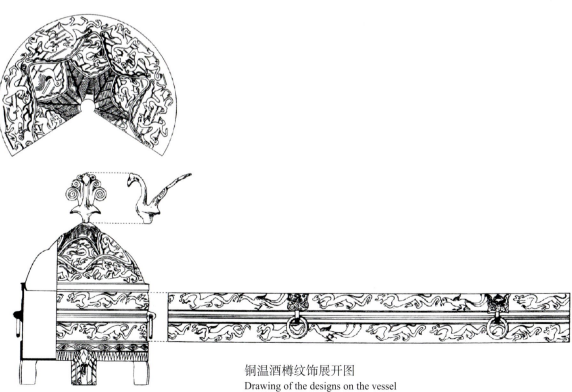

铜温酒樽纹饰展开图
Drawing of the designs on the vessel

四山铜镜，西汉，1982年柳园岗出土。
Bronze mirror with four motif, Western Han, from Liuyuangang in 1982.

规矩四灵镜，东汉，1953年龙生岗出土。镜以规矩、四灵纹为主，配
以羽人、小鸟、独角兽等。此镜为破镜，置于女棺内头部的漆匣中（男棺
被盗，镜已不存），广州南越墓已有用破镜随葬，由此得知人们意思中
"破镜重圆"的意愿在西汉初年已存在了。

Bronze mirror with four auspicious animals, Eastern Han, found from Longshenggang in
1953.

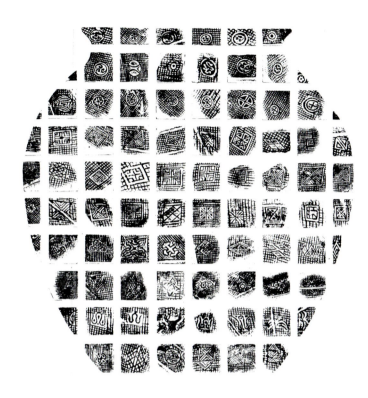

广州汉代陶器几何花纹拓本
Rubbing of geometric motifs on Han pottery wares found in Guangzhou

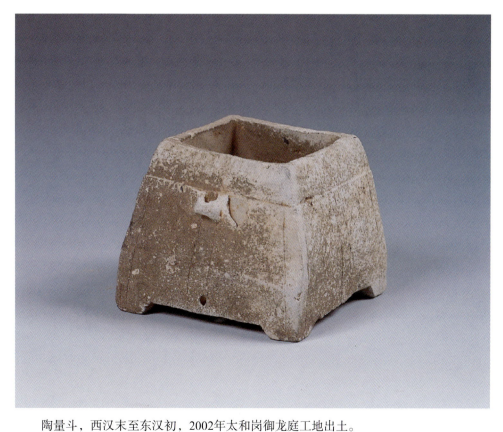

陶量斗，西汉末至东汉初，2002年太和岗御龙庭工地出土。
Pottery measuring unit for grain, *dou*, (1 *dou* =1 decalitre), dated back from the end of the Western Han to the early Eastern Han, excavated from the field of Yulongting, Taihegang in 2002.

陶砚，东汉，1955年先烈路出土。
Pottery ink stone, Eastern Han, from Xianlie Road in 1955.

黛砚、砚石，东汉，1953年龙生岗出土。汉代化妆用具，用黛墨放在砚上研磨，用眉笔蘸黛画眉。
Ink stone for grilling eyebrow pigment, Eastern Han, from Longshenggang in 1953. The black ink was grilled on the ink stone and painted by brush on eyebrows, popular in Han Dynasty.

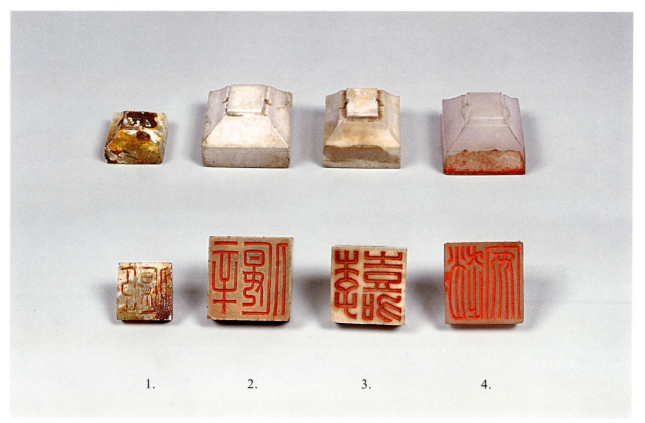

1. 　　2. 　　3. 　　4.

　　1.2、"臣偃""辛偃"玉印，西汉，1956年先烈路麻鹰岗出土。两印同出一墓。出土时与铁削刀、铁刮刀、鎏金铜指环共置于一漆奁内，漆奁已朽。

　　Jade stamp inscribed Xin Yan、Official Yan，Western Han, from Mayinggang, Xianlie Road in 1956. Both stamps were found from the same tomb, supposedly belonged to one person, the tomb owner Han official Xin Yan. Both of them were originally found in a decayed lacquer make-up box, along with a gilt copper ring, iron cutter and iron scraper.

　　3."李嘉"玉印，西汉，1955年华侨新村岘壳岗出土。正方形，复斗钮，刻篆文"李嘉"二字。

　　Jade stamp inscribed Lee Jia, Western Han, from Xiankegang, Huaqiaoxincun in 1955. Shaped in square with an upside-down knob.

　　4."赵安"玛瑙印，西汉，1955年华侨新村玉子岗出土。正方形，复斗钮，刻篆体文"赵安"二字。

　　Agate stamp inscribed Zhao An in bronze carving scripts，Western Han, from Yuzigang, Huaqiaoxincun in 1955. Shaped in square with an upside-down knob.

陶鼓，西汉，1986年农林下路出土。
Pottery drum, Western Han, from Nonglinxia Road in 1986.

陶烛台，东汉，2003年执信中学工地出土。器体分立柱和承盆两部分，可以判定这是点烛而非燃油的灯台，惜至今汉墓仍未有蜡烛出土。

Pottery candle base，Eastern Han, from the field of Zhixin High School in 2003. It has a standing pillar and a candle support plate. It can be identified as for burning candlewick not for oil wick, but so far the Han period candle has not been found ye.

　　铜鎏金跪坐俑，西汉，1956年麻鹰岗出土。通体鎏金，大部分已脱落。发型为朝天髻，身着交领右襟长服，跪坐，双手按于腹前。疑为墓主以侍俑从殉。

Copper female figurine gilded in gold, Western Han, from Mayinggang in 1956. The figurine was fully gilded in gold, but now some traces are left only. With her hair tied up highly, she wears long robe with chest panel opening to the right, kneeling with hands rested on tummy. This figurine could be acting as the servant of the tomb owner to be buried aside.

陶舞俑，东汉后期，1955年先烈路出土。舞俑身着长袖宽衣和长裙，束腰，衣饰华丽，服饰上原施彩绘，除裙脚花边尚存外，余已脱落。长裙呈喇叭筒形，曳地。作浓妆打扮。头上结三丫髻，插五簪，贴花钿。两耳带菊花形耳环。舞俑右手在前，左手反旋于后，作歌舞姿态。

Pottery dancing figurine, late Eastern Han, unearthed from Xianlie Road in 1955. The dancer wears long robe with loose sleeves and long skirt down to the floor, and a tight belt around waist. The rainbow like costume was painted magnificently yet now fragmented. The dancer wears heavy make-up, with tied hair in shape of three "Y", decorated with five head pins, and sticking flowers on face. Earrings in chrysanthemum shaped. She puts her right hand in front and left hand behind back, twisting and dancing.

陶乐俑，东汉，1955年先烈路出土。这组乐俑与陶舞俑同出一墓中。三俑组成一组，一人在拨弦弹奏，二人击掌为节，作伴奏姿态。
Pottery figurine of musicians, late Eastern Han, unearthed from Xianlie Road in 1955, along with the above-mentioned dancing figurine from the same tomb. One musician is playing a music instrument while the other two are clapping aside.

陶俑，东汉，1956年广州先烈路出土。
Pottery figurines, Eastern Han, unearthed from Xianlie Road in 1956.

陶牛车，东汉，1954年黄花岗出土。汉代，席蓬顶牛车通常为贵族或士人所用，盛行于东汉时期。

Pottery ox-cart, Eastern Han, discovered in 1954 from Huanghuagang. This type of Ox-cart with canopy was popular in Han period, used by Han nobles and literati.

陶马车，东汉，1955年先烈路出土。

Pottery chariot, Eastern Han, discovered in 1955 from Xianlie Road.

干栏式陶屋，西汉后期，1953年先烈路龙生岗出土。分上下二层，上为人居，下养牲畜。上层前面为横形正堂，左侧后附廊屋，作厕所。悬山式屋顶，高低脊构成曲尺形。前墙右边开门口，左边开窗，上为直棂，下作菱格式。下层的基座有两面镂空舞像。后院畜圈有高墙围绕，墙根设有窦洞，方便守门犬进出。

Pottery model of two-storey farmhouse, Late Western Han, from Longshenggang, Xianlie Road in 1953. The two-storey dwelling houses the family upstairs, and the animals below and in the yard. The upper floor has a front hall and a side toilet on the left wing, The vaulted roof has its high and low parts in zigzag shape. The door opens at front right and window on the left are decorated in vertical lines and diamond wooden pieces. On the base incised dancing figures are depicted on both sides. The back yard is a cattle pen surrounded by high walls, while a dog hole is designed at the root of the wall for the door guardian dog.

陶屋门上画像拓本

干栏式陶屋，东汉前期，1953年先烈路龙生岗出土。通体施黄褐色釉。上层平面曲尺形，前部是通堂，左后室作厕间。门口设在前墙的左边，双扇门，半掩，门板上划有图像，应为《后汉书·礼仪志》所说的"门神"。

Pottery model of two-storey farmhouse, Early Eastern Han, from Dragon- rising Hillock, Xianlie Road in 1953. The model is fully covered in yellowish brown glaze. The upper floor is shaped in zigzag, with a front hall and a side room on the left as a toilet. At the front wall two doors are half opening. On the door a pair of door guardian divinities is depicted, as described in *Hou Han Shu* (History of the Later Han Dynasty), Chapter of Ritual.

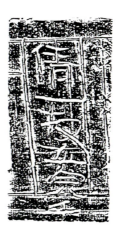

陶屋门上铭文拓本

曲尺式陶屋，东汉前期，1956年海珠区大元岗出土。曲尺形屋，上盖三脊四坡，坡面平缓。正屋为横堂，门口开左边，右边开窗。横堂右边后侧的上层是厕间。后侧相对的两面用矮墙围起成后院，用作饲养牲畜的圈栏。廊屋的旁门上刻写"倩封墓"三字。

Pottery model of zigzag cottage, early Eastern Han, recovered from Dayuangang, Haizhu District in 1956. The zigzag cottage has a main hall and a side chamber, with three vaulted roofs and four leaping ceilings. underneath the cottage is the horizontal front Hall, with door opens on the left and windows on the right. The toilet is at the upper floor on the right. In the back yard there is a cattle pen surrounded by low walls. The door is inscribed by "tomb of Qian Feng".

三合式陶屋，东汉后期，1955年先烈路出土。前为堂屋，内有俑在舂米、簸米。两廊屋在后边。廊屋后墙间用矮墙围成后院。悬山式屋盖。左边廊屋作厕所，右边廊屋为畜舍。舍门外边架一斜梯，四只山羊正鱼贯而入。

Pottery model of hermitage, Late Eastern Han, from Xianlie Road in 1955. Two figurines are grilling and winnowing rice in the front hall, behind whick are two side chambers. The back yard is surrounded by short fence. The roof is in "A" shape. The left wing ear room is toilet, and the right one is cowshed. A ladder case is leaning by the door. Four goats are going home one by one.

陶望楼，东汉，1957年西村出土。
Pottery watching tower，Eastern Han, from Stone Hillock, West Village, in 1957.

　　楼阁式陶屋，东汉前期，1957年东山象栏岗出土。汉墓出土的楼阁式陶屋，形式多样，结构复杂而富于变化。楼阁式陶屋以此规模最大。结构严整，布局均衡，有明显的中轴线，在整个建筑的组合上高低参错，主次分明，说明中国建筑以木构架为结构骨架，以中轴线为基础的对称布局形式，到汉代已完全成熟。

Pottery model of multi-story Pavilion, Early Eastern Han, discovered from Xianglangang, Dongshan in 1957. Among different types of pottery pavilions recovered from Han tombs, this piece is the biggest. It has symmetric structure and versatile decorations, with a clear axis, demonstrating that during the Han Dynasty, the wooden structure architecture in symmetric design had been mature in China.

　　陶城堡，东汉后期，1956年广州东山三育路出土。平面方形，高墙围绕四周，前后大门都在中轴线上，大门口各有一员文吏和执兵武士守卫。门上建四阿顶城楼，四隅设角楼。城堡之内有两幢长方形陶屋，其中一幢分上下二层，旁设楼梯，左侧是厕所。城堡内有众多的家兵武装、侍卫、奴婢、歌舞乐俑、工匠、农奴，有的端坐，有的跪拜等，情态各异。

　　Pottery citadel, Late Eastern Han, from Sanyu Road, Dongshan, Guangzhou in 1956. Shaped in square, surrounded by high wall, with front and back gates located on the central line, guarded with one civil official and one armed warrior. Four pavilions are built at the castle gate, and four watching towers at each corner. Inside the castle there are two rectangular houses. One is two storey with staircase, and a toilet on the left side. Many pottery figurines are depicted as warriors, male servants, maids, musicians, craftsmen, farming slaves sitting, kneeling or standing in various gestures.

　　陶船，东汉，1954年沙河顶出土。这是一艘航行于内河兼浅海岸的客货两用船。船分前中后三舱。船尾有望楼。船前系锚，后有舵。船头两边安插浆架三根，舱内横架梁担八条，以加强船体结构的牢固及加深吃水量。从它的规模结构来看，说明广州人民在造船方面已掌握了高超技术。"舵"的发明是我国古代人民对世界造船史的一大贡献。

　　Pottery boat, Eastern Han(25AD-220AD). Unearthed in 1954 from Shaheding site, suitable for carrying people and cargo navigating on river and sea. It has three cabins, one at the front, one in the middle, one at the stern equipped with a watching tower. The anchor is in the front and the rudder is in the rear chamber. On each side of the prow there are three oars, and eight horizontal wooden corbels to reinforce the cabins and made the vessel heavier and go deeper into water. Judging from the large scale and scientific structure of the boat, it seems local people had a superior navigation technique over 2000 years ago. The innovation of rudder was Chinese important contribution to the world navigation history.

陶船，东汉，1997年先烈中路凯城华庭工地出土。（广州市文物考古研究所提供）
Pottery boat，Eastern Han，discovered in 1997 from Xianlie Road. (provided by the Cultural Relics and Archaeological Research Institution of Guangzhou)

自日南障塞、徐聞、合浦船行可五月，有都元國；又船行可四月，有邑盧沒國；又船行可二十餘日，有諶離國；（一）步行可十餘日，有夫甘都盧國。（二）自夫甘都盧國船行可二月餘，有黃支國，民俗略與珠厓相類。其州廣大，戶口多，多異物，自武帝以來皆獻見。有譯長，屬黃門，與應募者俱入海市明珠、璧流離、奇石異物，齎黃金雜繒而往。所至國皆稟食為耦，（三）蠻夷賈船，轉送致之。亦利交易，剽殺人~（四）又苦逢風波溺死，不者數年來還。大珠至圍二寸以下。平帝元始中，王莽輔政，欲燿威德，厚遺黃支王，令遣使獻生犀牛。自黃支船行可八月，到皮宗；船行可（八）二月，到日南、象林界云。黃支之南，有已程不國，漢之譯使自此還矣。

《汉书·地理志》记载，汉武帝时派遣使节远航至黄支国（印度建志补罗）等地，进行贸易和友好往来。

According to *Han Shu, Chapter of Geography*, emperor Wudi sent envoy to travel as far as Huangzhi port in India for trade and diplomatic activities.

蓝色玻璃碗，西汉，1954年登峰路横枝岗出土。此碗为舶来品，产自古罗马帝国。
Blue glass bowl, Western Han, discovered in 1954, Dengfeng Road, Hengzhigang, originally from the Roman Empire.

陶象牙，西汉，1960年马棚岗出土。其造型取材于非洲象牙。同墓共出土15件犀角，说明汉代的番禺是海外进口货物的集散地。

Pottery models of elephant tusks, Western Han, discovered in 1960 from Mapenggang, shaped in African elephant tusks. 15 pieces of rhinoceros horns were found beside them, showing that Panyu (Ancient Guangzhou) was the exchange spot for exotic articles during the Han period.

陶犀角，西汉，1953年梅花村出土。
Pottery models of rhinoceros horns, Western Han, from Meihuacun in 1953.

　　铜熏炉，西汉，1956年黄花岗出土。熏炉是熏香用具，香料产自海外。广州汉墓出土了大量熏炉，一方面反映熏香已成为贵族生活的一种习尚，另一方面说明广州海外贸易发达。

　　Bronze incense burner, Western Han, from Huanghuagang in 1956. Dramatically, a considerable number of incense burner were discovered from Han tombs in Guangzhou, indicating that as early as the Han period aristocrats in South China had already enjoyed exotic incenses such as murr, frankincense, sandalwood etc. in their daily lives. On the other hand, it testifies to the prosperity of the maritime trade in Guangzhou at that time.

陶熏炉，西汉，1955年华侨新村出土。
Bronze censer, Western Han, from Huaqiaoxincun in 1955.

水晶玛瑙珊瑚珠串，东汉，1955年龙生岗出土。珠串上有金狮球、水晶、珊瑚及用药物饰花的玛瑙。这些装饰品为佩带之用，应是当时由海路输入到广州的。

String of pearl beads mixed with crystal, agate and carol, Eastern Han, from Longshenggang in 1955. It is decorated with gold lion ball, crystal, carol, agate decorated with herbs. As luxury ornament, it was supposedly imported by sea via Guangzhou.

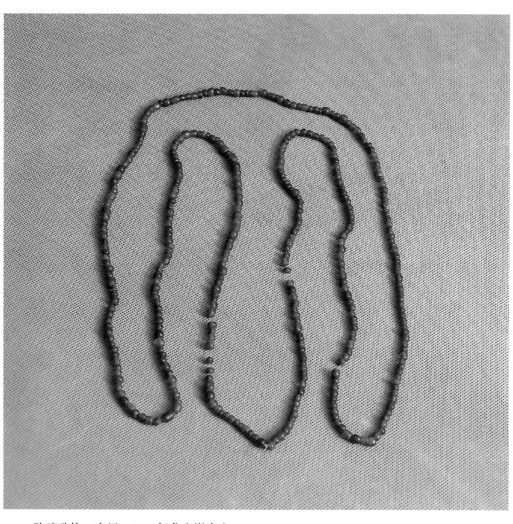

琉璃珠饰，东汉，1953年龙生岗出土。
A string of beads made of colored glaze, Eastern Han, from Longshenggang in 1953.

　　陶俑座灯，西汉后期（前32~24年），1955年大元岗出土。在广州，这种用奴隶形象为座的陶灯，从西汉武帝以后开始出现。早期，俑体消瘦；东汉晚期，俑几乎尽是体态肥胖的。这件陶灯的灯奴，屈膝蹲坐，左手斜托灯盘，右手支于腿上，仰首注视。

Pottery lamp supported by slave figure, late Western Han (32BC-8AD), from Dayuangang in 1955. This type of pottery lamp appeared since the reign of emperor Wudi when the Silk Road was newly opened. It has a couple of categories: the early slaves are very thin; and the late ones have chubby-checks. On this piece the Central Asian looking slave sit on his kneeling legs, looking upwards, with left hand holding the lamp basin, and right hand putting on the leg.

　　陶俑座灯，东汉后期，2001年下塘西路狮带岗出土。（广州市文物考古研究所提供）

Pottery lamp supported by slave figure, late Eastern Han (76-220), from Shidaigang, Xiatangxi Road in 2001. (provided by the Cultural Relics and Archaeological Research Institution of Guangzhou)

陶俑座灯，东汉后期，1999年先烈南路大宝岗出土。俑为胡人脸形，眼睛细长，高鼻梁，尖长下巴，连腮胡子，头发束于脑后折向前成髻。（广州市文物考古研究所提供）
Pottery lamp supported by slave figure, late Eastern Han (76-220), from Dabaogang, Xianlienan Road in 1999. The figurine is of Central Asian appearance, with thin and long eyes, shaped nose and shaped chain, heavy beard, with hair tired up. (Provided by the Cultural Relics and Archaeological Research Institution of Guangzhou)

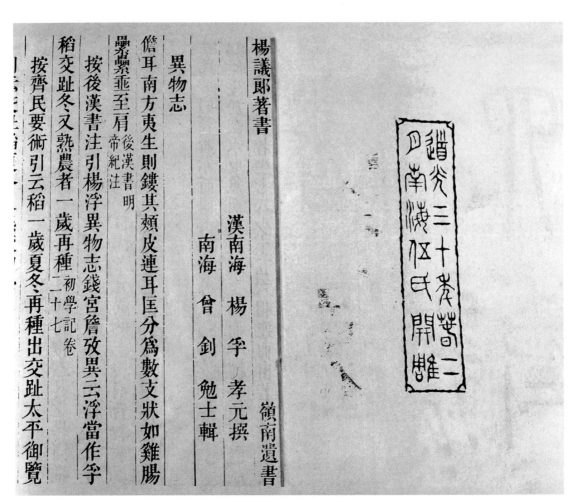

《异物志》，东汉杨孚撰。书中记载了南方的动植物、水产、工艺等，对研究古代南方的风土物产有重要的参考价值。原书失传，《岭南遗书》辑载其中片断。

Yiwuzhi (Annuals of Strange Things), by Yangfu in the Eastern Han Dynasty. Fauna, flora, aquatic product, as well as arts and crafts in the South China are recorded in this book, which is of great importance to the research of the ancient natural conditions and products in South China. Unfortunately, the original book was lost, and only parts were compiled in *Lingnan Yishu* (Remained Book of Lingnan)

广州得名
Naming Guangzhou

三国东吴黄武五年，即公元226年，东吴将交州划为交、广二州分治，广州由此得名，州治番禺。从三国至南北朝时期，北方战乱频繁，而广州社会稳定，北方人民大量南迁，带来了先进的文化和技术，直接推动了广州经济文化的发展。

In 226 AD（Three Kingdoms period）, Jiaozhou state （which covers Lingnan region） under the Wu kingdom was divided into Jiaozhou and Guangzhou. Canton was called Guangzhou state ever since, centered in Panyu. From then to the Northern and Southern Dynasties, Guangzhou was in a long time peace; meanwhile, it accepted a large number of migrants escaped from the chaotic North China. These migrants brought exquisite culture and technique to Guangzhou.

三国时期吴国交、广州分治图
Map of Jiaozhou and Guangzhou state during the Three Kingdoms period

陸遜督諸將大破休於石亭大司馬呂範卒是歲改合

太守周魴僞叛誘魏將曹休秋八月權至皖口使將軍

七年春三月封子慮爲建昌侯罷東安郡夏五月鄱陽

六年春正月諸將獲彭綺閏月韓當子琮以其衆降魏

分交州置廣州俄復舊爲江表傳曰權於武昌新裝大船名

中褚逢齋以就遜及諸葛瑾意所不安令損益之是歲

免此實其心所望於君也於是令有司盡寮有儀使郎

重稷之自此以後不復名之常呼曰谷爲貴

稷何於是以死爭權於谷利利輒敢以死爭權於谷利是

於不測之中船樓茇高邈近顛危岌岌社

乃還權曰大王萬乘之主輕

工曰不取樊口阿利卽轉柂入樊口風遂猛不可行

谷利令柂工取樊口者斬工卽羅州利技刀向柂

免此實其心所望於君也於是令有司盡寮有儀使郎

《三国志·吴·孙权传》中记载，东吴黄武五年（226年），孙权分交州合浦以北为广州，广州得名。

According to *San Guo Zhi* (History of the Three Kingdoms Period), Sun Quan of the Wu Kingdom designated the area to the south of Hepu as Jiaozhou and the area to its north as Guangzhou. The term "Guangzhou" appeared at the first time.

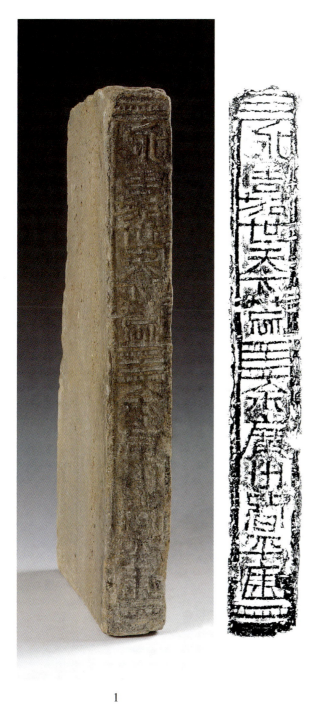

1

2

晋代墓砖，广州出土。铭文显示当时的广州社会安定。
Tomb bricks of the Jin Dynasty, the inscription shows that the Guangzhou
society was in peace and the economy was flourishing.
铭文：1、永嘉世，天下荒，余广州，皆平康。
2、永嘉世，九州空，余吴土，盛且丰。

1

2

晋代墓砖，1954年西村矻岗出土。
Tomb bricks in the Jin Dynasty, excavated from the Magang,
Xicun, in 1954
　　铭文：1、永嘉中，天下灾，但江南，皆康平。
　　　　　2、永嘉七年癸酉皆宜价市。

　　东汉、晋、南朝城墙遗址，位于中山五路原艳芳照相馆所在地，1996年夏发掘。残长16米，南北走向。遗址始建于东汉，晋代和南朝扩建沿用。东晋时，以东汉墙体为芯扩宽夯筑加固，以向上收分的方式砌筑。在外墙基础部分发现有砖模印"泰元十一年"（东晋武帝司马耀"太元"年号，十一年即386年，"泰"与"太"通）字样，为筑墙年代。（广州市文物考古研究所提供）

City wall ruins of the Eastern Han, the Jin and Southern Dynasties (220 ~ 581), at the location of Yanfang photo studio, Zhongshanwu Road, excavated in summer in 1996. The exposed part is 16m in length, in south-north direction. This part of the city wall was firstly built in the Eastern Han, and inherited and enlarged in Jin and Southern Dynasties. Based on the Han city wall, Jin people thicken the wall by yellowish red bricks, in method of going up and up . The remained wall is 7.6 m wide atop and 8.8 m wide at the bottom, 1.4 m high. On the base of the outer-wall some bricks inscribed "the elevnth year of Taiyuan era", which help archaeologists to date precisely the outer-wall was built in 386AD during the Eastern Jin period. (provided by the Cultural Relics and Archaeological Research Institution of Guangzhou)

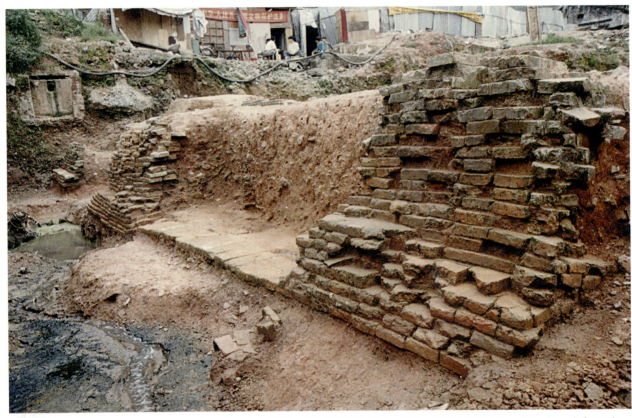

南朝城墙遗址，1996年中山五路发现。南朝城墙在晋砖城两边填土扩宽，墙壁包砖砌筑。宽21米、残高1.5米。在西侧还发现一处马面结构，构筑形式与墙体相同。南朝墙体的西、东两侧分别有唐代和宋代的路面、水池遗迹，表明此城墙到唐代已废弃。（广州市文物考古研究所提供）

Ruins of City Wall of Southern Dynasties, found at Zhongshanwu Road in 1996. It filled the Jin city wall by soils, and padded with bricks on both sides. The exposed part is 21m wide and remained 1.5m high. The zigzag wall structure, the so-called "horse face", was discovered at the western side, in south-north direction, 9.1m long and 7.3m wide in the northern side and 8.1 m wide in the southern side. The structure was built in the same method as the city wall, and celadon bowl and brown grazed jar were recovered here. On both side of the city wall, the site of water pool and high road dated in Tang and Song time, indicating that up to Tang Dynasty, this part of the city wall had been abandoned. (provided by the Cultural Relics and Archaeological Research Institution of Guangzhou)

三国时期铜钱窖藏遗址，2000年11月发现于西湖路广州百货大楼新翼工地，出土有大泉五百、大泉二千、大泉当千等铜钱，重量达三四百斤。（广州市文物考古研究所提供）

Site of storage of bronze coins, Three Kingdoms Period (220 ~ 265), discovered at the site of Guangzhou Department Store in West Lake in November, 2000. Among coins the most striking items are Daquan 500, Daquan 1000 and Daquan 2000, which is around 150 ~ 200 kg in total. (provided by the Cultural Relics and Archaeological Research Institution of Guangzhou)

上：大泉二千铜钱；下：大泉当千铜钱，2000年西湖路广州百货大楼出土。（广州市文物考古研究所提供）
The huge bronze coins, include Daquanerqian and Daquandangqian, Three Kingdoms Period（220～265），discovered at the field of Guangzhou Department Store on Xihu Road in 2000. (provided by the Cultural Relics and Archaeological Research Institution of Guangzhou)

1974年在中山四路发现一处规模较大的东晋冶铁遗址，存有大量烧土、铁渣、炉底基石等，与《晋书》广州"大开鼓铸"的记载相印证。

Remains of a large-scale smeltery in the Eastern Jin period found in Zhongshansi Road in 1974. Large amount of burnt clay, scoria and foot stones of the stove were found in this site, verifying the records of thriving smelting industry in Guangzhou in *Jinshu* (History of the Jin Dynasty).

陶牛栏，晋永嘉年间，1994年黄埔区姬堂3号墓出土。圈栏由14根直柱绕成一圆圈构成。开一门，单扇向里掩，一俑正推门入内。圈内有大小水牛四只。（广州市文物考古研究所提供）

Cattle pen，Yongjia era (307 ~ 312 AD), Jin Dynasty, excavated from Jitang tomb No. 3, Whampoa District in 1994. It is a circle made of 14 wooden pillars. A servant figurine is opening the door and walking in to feed four buffaloes. (provided by the Cultural Relics and Archaeological Research Institution of Guangzhou)

陶鸡屋，晋永嘉年间，1994年黄埔区姬堂2号墓出土。屋舍呈长方形，室内当中用墙分隔为左右两舍。右舍养鸡，一俑站在食槽边投放饲料。舍内有五只鸡，其中两只在槽边进食，一只在后墙根伏地休息，还有两只上下相叠在交配中。左舍养猪，一俑站食槽前，正在给2猪喂养。（广州市文物考古研究所提供）

Pottery cattle pen, dated in Yongjia era (307 ~ 312 AD), Jin dynasty, discovered in 1994, tomb No.2, Jitang, Huangpu District. The house is in shape of rectangular with vaulted roof made of rice stem. It has two rooms with doors opened but no window. In the room on the right side, a servant figurine is feeding chicken by the trough, while two chicken are eating, one is resting, other two are mating. In the left room, a servant figurine is feeding two pigs. (provided by the Cultural Relics and Archaeological Research Institution of Guangzhou)

陶囷，晋永嘉年间（307～312年），1994年黄埔区姬堂2号墓出土。囷体圆形，下为方形基座。开一长方形门口，周边有凸起门框，单扇门，一俑在里面正将门打开。盖顶呈圆锥形高起，中间呈尖柱状，坡面遍划线纹以示为稻秆所盖。囷体亦划斜方格等线纹，表示壁系由竹笪围绕而成。（广州市文物考古研究所提供）

Pottery granary, Yongjia era (307～312AD), Jin Dynasty, discovered in 1994, tomb No.3, Jitang, Huangpu District. The granary is shaped in round on a square base. The door is rectangular with relief door flame, while a figure servant is opening the door from inside. The roof is covered by straw sterns. The cover is shaped in pyramid. The wall of the granary is carved by diamond motif, showing that it was made of bamboo sterns. (provided by the Cultural Relics and Archaeological Research Institution of Guangzhou)

陶水井，晋永嘉年间（307～312年），1994年黄埔区姬堂3号墓出土。井体圆筒形，子口形成井栏，底部向里收削一圈。一戴冠俑站井栏旁提水，一手扶栏，一手握绳。长绳及井底，连着一个提梁的汲水斗。春秋战国时对井绳与水斗称为"绠、缶"，《左传·襄公九年》有"具绠缶，备水器"记载。《荀子·荣辱》有"短绠不可以汲深井之泉"记载。（广州市文物考古研究所提供）

Pottery well, Yongjia era (307～312 AD), Jin dynasty, discovered in 1994, tomb No.3, Jitang, Huangpu District. The well is shaped in cylinder, with narrow rim. A figurine wearing tiara is gathering water beside the well rail, with arope in one hand. The rope is very long and deeply prolong into the well, with a water container with a handle in the end. This type of well rope and water basket was recorded as early as the Spring and Autumn Period(881BC～576BC), both mentioned by historic books entitled *Zuo Zhuan* and *Xun Zi*. (provided by the Cultural Relics and Archaeological Research Institution of Guangzhou)

　　陶灶，晋永嘉年间（307～312年），1994年黄埔区姬堂2号墓出土。灶身前广后敛束，平面近似三角形。灶壁呈拱形。灶面开两个灶眼，上置2釜1甑。灶门大敞，前有地台伸出，1俑站地台上烧火。灶膛内有燃柴2根。（广州市文物考古研究所提供）

　　Pottery cooking stove, dated in Yongjia era (307～312AD), Jin Dynasty, discovered in 1994, tomb No.3, Jitang, Huangpu District. The cooking stove is wide in the front and narrow in the rear. It has two cooking pits, on which are two pots and one pan. The stove door is open, with a plat form in fornt where a figurine is making fire.(provided by the Cultural Relics and Archaeological Research Institution of Guangzhou)

　　陶水田，晋永嘉年间（307～312年），1994年黄埔区姬堂2号墓出土。长方形，田亩中有"十"字形田埂分成大小同等的四块水田，田上刻划点纹和线纹，以示耕作后留的犁耙痕。田中有农夫（俑）使牛磨田（犁耙下压上一根长木，用牛牵引，以平整犁耙后高低不平的耕土才能莳田），有坐在田埂上修磨农具，有在牛头上缠牛绳，表示这块田已犁耙完毕，还有一块田，田上的俑与畜缺失，留下四个印痕。（广州市文物考古研究所提供）

　　Pottery paddy field, dated in Yongjia era (307 ~ 312AD), Jin Dynasty, discovered in 1994, from Jitang tomb No. 2, Whampoa District in 1994. Shaped in rectangular, divided evenly into four pieces by a cross, where dots and lines showing the traces after ploughing. Several farmer figurines are depicted, one guiding the bull to flat the farm before planting, one sitting to repair the tools, one finishing the plough by tiding a robe on the bull head. In the last piece of the farm, the farmer and bull figurines have vanished but left traces.(provided by the Cultural Relics and Archaeological Research Institution of Guangzhou)

青釉槅，晋永嘉年间（307～312年），
1994年黄埔区姬堂3号墓出土。长方形高身
盒，有子口，无盖，盆中隔分为三行共九格，
下连拱形座。江西南昌晋墓出有漆槅，底有漆
书"吴氏槅"。槅在全国南北各地的晋墓都
有发现，是具有时代特点的器形。（广州市文
物考古研究所提供）

Celadon box, dated to Yongjia era (307 ~ 312 AD),
Jin Dynasty, from Jitang tomb No. 3, Whampoa District in
1994. Deep container in rectangular shape, without cover
but a inner rim, divided into 9 parts in 3 lines, on a arched
base. A similar sample is a lacquer container found from Jin
tomb in Nanchang, Jiangxi province, inscribed by
lacquer "Hé of Wu family". This type of celadon
container is a typical Jin ware, which can be found widely
from Jin tombs all around China, providing an identical
dating. (provided by the Cultural Relics and Archaeological
Research Institution of Guangzhou)

青釉四耳罐，晋永嘉年间（307～312年），
1994年黄埔区姬堂3号墓出土。（广州市文物考古研究
所提供）

Celadon covered container and four-lugged jar, Yongjia era
(307 ~ 312 AD), Jin Dynasty, excavated from Jitang tomb No. 3,
Whampoa District in 1994. (provided by the Cultural Relics and
Archaeological Research Institution of Guangzhou)

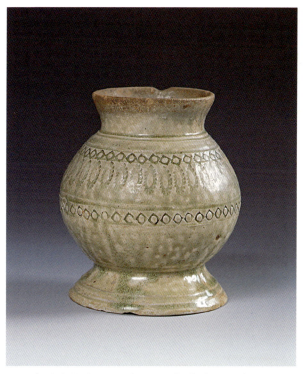

青釉印纹壶，西晋，1994年黄埔区姬堂3号墓出
土。（广州市文物考古研究所提供）

Celadon jar with impressed decoration, Western Jin, excavated
from No.3 Jitang tomb, Whampoa District in 1994. (provided by the
Cultural Relics and Archaeological Research Institution of Guangzhou)

青釉熏炉，南朝，三元里出土。
Celadon censer, Southern Dynasties, excavated from Sanyuanli.

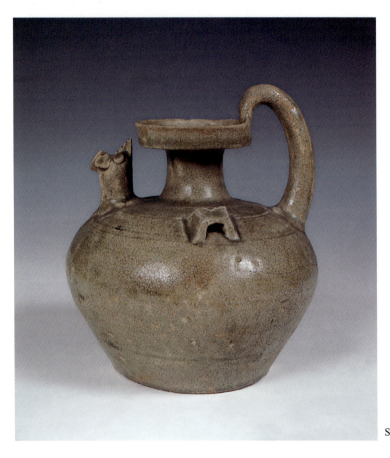

青釉鸡首壶，西晋，1981年沙河顶出土。
Celadon chicken headed kettle, Western Jin, from Shaheding in 1981.

印花三足罐，晋，1955年桂花岗出土。
Pottery Jar with three feet and stamped pattern, Jin Dynasty, from Guihuagang in 1955.

青釉水注，晋，1955年桂花岗出土。
Celadon waterspout, Jin Dynasty, from Guihuagang in 1955.

青釉虎子，西晋，1981年沙河顶出土。
Celadon waterspout，Western Jin，from Shaheding in 1981.

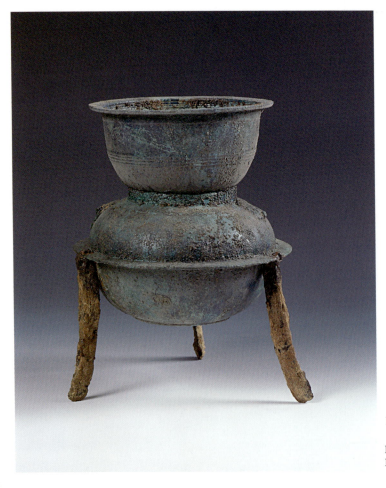

铜甑，晋永嘉年间（307～312年），1994年黄埔区姬堂墓出土。
Bronze vase, Yongjia era（307～312AD）, Jin Dynasty, discovered in 1994, tomb of Jitang, Whampoa District.

陶牛车，西晋，1981年沙河顶出土。
Pottery ox-cart, Western Jin , from Shaheding in 1981.

骑马俑，西晋，1981年沙河顶出土。
Pottery figurine on horse back，Western Jin，from Shaheding in 1981.

部曲将印，东晋，1953年龙生岗出土。
Stamp of general Buqu, Eastern Jin, from Longshenggang in 1953.

六面铜印，南朝（420～589年），1955年华南工学院出土。
Bronze stamp carved on six faceted，Southern Dynasties(420～589AD), excavated from
the Huanan Institute of Technology in 1955.

滑石猪，晋，1955年沙河顶出土。
Talcum piglet，Western Jin，from Shaheding in 1956.

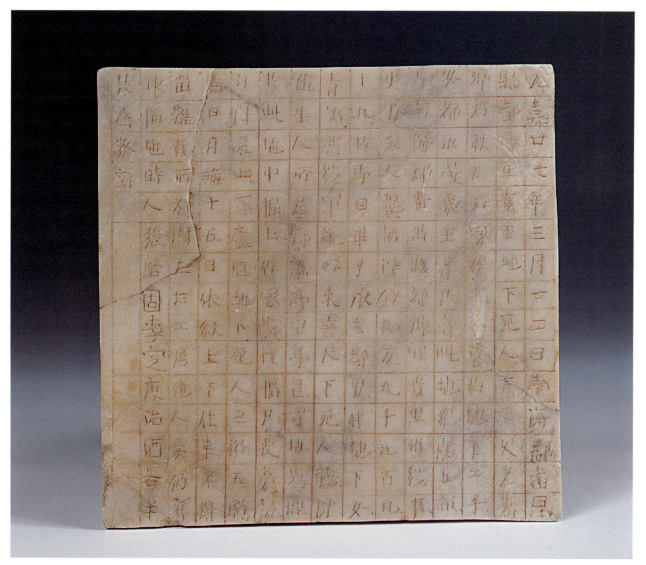

滑石买地券，南朝（420～589年），2004年淘金东路中星小学工地出土。这是广州地区首次发现的南朝买地券。共有214字。字体介于隶楷之间，刻写较随意。（广州市文物考古研究所提供）

Talcum stele, contract of buying a real property，Southern Dynasties(420～589AD), unearthed from Zhongxing Primary School at Taojin Road in 2004. According to present knowledge, it is the first time to discover a contract of buying a real property as early as Southern Dynasties in Guangzhou. It is 214 words in total, roughly carved in printing form calligraphy on talcum stele. (provided by the Cultural Relics and Archaeological Research Institution of Guangzhou)

121

虞翻（164～233年），会稽人。三国时被孙权贬广州，居虞苑并讲学，注《周易注十卷》。

Annotation to Zhouyi (Book of Changes), Volume 10, by Yufan in Huiji, who was relegated to Guangzhou by Sun Quan during the Three Kingdoms Period. He then stayed and gave lectures in the Yu Academy.

东晋隆安五年（401年），罽宾国（今克什米尔）法师昙摩耶舍来到广州建制旨寺（今光孝寺）大殿，传教译经。

In the year of 401, Buddhist master Dharmayasas came to Guangzhou by sea from Jinbin (present Kashmiri) and built the Guangxiao Temple for preaching and translating sutras.

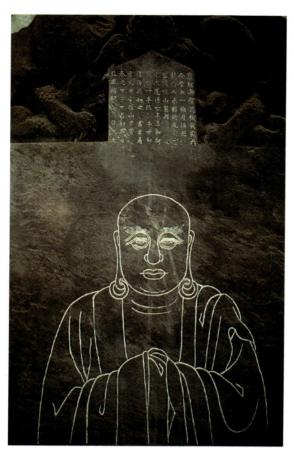

　　南粱普通八年（527年）印度僧达摩从海路来
到广州传教，成为中国佛教禅宗的初祖。图为光孝
寺内达摩像。

　　In the year of 527, Indian monk Bodhidharma arrived in
Guangzhou by sea. He became the first and the most influential
patriarch of Chan Buddhism in China. This is the portrait of
Bodhidharma.

　　达摩禅师在广州登陆处称为西来初地，并建西来
奄，清初改称华林寺。图为华林寺五百罗汉堂。

　　The celebrated Indian monk Bodhidharma established the Xilai'an in Guangzhou. The
spot where he landed came to be called xilai chudi (the first touching of land on journeying
from the west), which was later renamed Hualin Temple in the early Qing Dynasty. This is
the Vihara of Five-hundred Arhats inside the temple.

　　东晋，南海太守鲍靓为女儿鲍姑在越秀山麓建道观越冈院，明万历时改为三元宫（上图）。内有虬龙井，又称鲍姑井（下图）。鲍姑常用井水及井旁红艾为民治病。

　　Taoist Sanyuan Temple was built at the foot of the Yuexiu Mountain in the Eastern Jin period. There is a Bao Gu well inside. Legend has it that Bao often used the water in the well and the artemisia growing nearby to cure sickness for people.

天 子 南 庫

Imperial Treasury in the South

　　造船技术的提高与海外贸易的持续发展，使广州成为唐代"通海夷道"的起点。沿着这条当时世界上最长的远洋航线，外国商船纷纷抵达广州，海外奇珍异宝云集于此，进出口贸易空前繁荣。唐开元四年（716年），张九龄重修大庾岭路，使南北交通更为顺畅。广州成为唐代市舶贸易的重要口岸，也是中央王朝财政收入的重要来源，被时人誉为"天子南库"。这种局面一直持续到明清时期。

The technique of ocean-going shipbuilding in Guangzhou developed constantly, bringing in thriving overseas trade here during the Tang Dynasty (618~906). The Maritime Silk Road often started from the Guangzhou Harbour, followed the longest marine voyage line in the world during the Medieval Age, various foreign commercial boats arrived Guangzhou, brought all kinds of exotic treasures. In 716 AD, Tang official Zhang Jiuling rebuilt the road of Dayuling, providing better transport line for the South to the North. Guangzhou was the most important harbour for overseas trade in the Tang time, and one of the major financial incoming sources for the Tang court, the so-called "Imperial Treasury in the South" from the Tang Dynasty up to Ming and Qing Dynasties.

　　广州德政中路唐代码头遗址出土的木桩，为海内外商船舶岸栓系缆绳之用。在广州文明路丽都酒店也出土了唐代码头遗址。这些表明唐代广州城珠江岸边码头林立，为海内外商船云集之地。

　　Wooden base, discovered from the Tang wharf site, Dezhengzhong Road, Guangzhou, for sea boats tying ropes. Another wharf site was also excavated at Lidu Hotel, Wenming Road, Guangzhou. It reveals that in the Tang Dynasty lots of wharves existed along the Pearl River bank for the Maritime Silk Road trade.

公元8世纪中叶，阿曼著名航海家欧贝德驾着双桅三帆木船"苏哈尔"号，依靠风力航行两年后抵达广州，拓展了阿拉伯帝国和唐朝的海上贸易航道，为中国带来亚麻、毛毯、金属制品以及阿曼特产乳香。中国的丝绸、陶瓷等也销往阿拉伯地区。

In the middle of the eighth century, a famous marine adventurer, Al- Baid undertook a two-years voyage from Oman to Guangzhou. He travelled on a wooden ocean-going vessel with two masts and three sails, named "Sohar", which completely relying on monsoon. His voyage throws light on the maritime trade between the Arabic Empire and the Tang Dynasty, bringing Arabic linen, fur carpet, metalwork, and Oman frankincense to China; and carrying the luxury silk and porcelain from China on the way return.

　　南海神庙始建于公元594年，唐玄宗时册尊南海神为广利王，以后历朝皇帝都派官员到此祭拜，祈祷"海不扬波、交通畅利"。（广州市文物考古研究所提供）

Temple of Southern Sea God was firstly built in 594 AD. During the reign of Xuanzong (713～756) the Tang court honored the Southern Sea God as King Guangli, since then the sacrificial ceremony of it was held officially through age, in order to blessing the Southern Sea stay in peace and keeping the marine trade in flourishing. (provided by the Cultural Relics and Archaeological Research Institution of Guangzhou)

银质莲瓣印花高足杯，唐代。唐代银器的制作工艺非常高超，有些银器通过广州出口到日本、东南亚等国。

Silver cup printed in lotus motif with high foot, Tang Dynasty. Influenced by West Asia and Central Asia metal works, silver wares in Tang China was superior and exported to Japan and Southeast Asia via Guangzhou harbor.

金质菊花小盏，宋代。
Golden calyx with chrysanthemum motif, Song Dynasty.

海兽葡萄纹铜镜，唐代。海兽葡萄纹镜主要流行于武则天时期，采用浮雕的工艺使画面高低起伏，呈强烈的立体感。瑞兽与葡萄的纹饰源自古代的波斯、拜占庭或希腊、罗马等地，六朝时开始在中国流行。铜镜不仅是唐人喜爱的日用品，亦是唐宋时期的出口商品。

Bronze mirror with sea lion and grape motif, Tang Dynasty. This type of bronze mirror was cherished in the reign of Emporess Wu (682 ~ 704). Using high relief technique，its sea lion and grape motifs are borrowed from Persia, Byzantium or Roman Empire, which became popular from the Southern Dynasties (420 ~ 581). Bronze mirror with a knob is a cute daily ware for Tang people, also highly appreciated by surrounding countries such as Japan and Korea in Tang and Song Dynasties.

端溪箕形砚,唐代。这是我国考古发现最完整最早的一块端溪砚。箕形砚是唐砚的常见样式,形同簸箕,靠近砚首部位有凹槽,以便贮存墨汁。又因砚尾端两侧向外撇似风字形,亦称风字形砚。

Ink stone shaped in dustpan, made in Duanxi, Tang Dynasty. This is the earliest and best preserved piece of ink stone made in Duanxi in China from archaeological discoveries. The ink stone shaped in winnowfan was popular in Tang Dynasty, with a part near the head is concaved to store ink. Since its ink stone tail is shaped like a Chinese script "wind". It is also called "wind" shape ink stone.

端溪抄手砚,宋代。
Ink stone made in Duanxi called "Chaoshou", Song Dynasty.

重修天庆观记碑刻拓片，北宋。碑文记述了宋代三佛齐国（今印度尼西亚）和宋王朝的友好往来，三佛齐商人捐资重修广州天庆观的事迹。

Stele rubbing of rebuilding Tianqing Guan Temple, Northern Song Dynasty. It records that Sanfoji Kingdom (modern Indonesia) had a touching friendship with Song court, and merchants from Sanfoji donated money to rebuilt the Tianqin Guan Temple in Guangzhou.

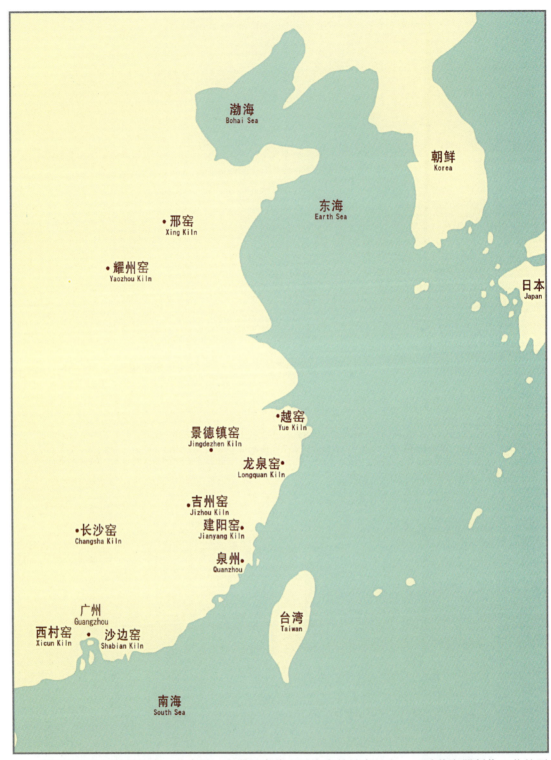

渤海
Bohai Sea

朝鲜
Korea

东海
Earth Sea

•邢窑
Xing Kiln

•耀州窑
Yaozhou Kiln

日本
Japan

•越窑
Yue Kiln

景德镇窑
Jingdezhen Kiln

龙泉窑
Longquan Kiln

•吉州窑
Jizhou Kiln

建阳窑
Jianyang Kiln

•长沙窑
Changsha Kiln

泉州•
Quanzhou

广州
Guangzhou

台湾
Taiwan

西村窑
Xicun Kiln

•沙边窑
Shabian Kiln

南海
South Sea

　　唐宋时期沿海外销瓷窑口分布图。瓷器是唐代以后大宗外销商品之一，随着瓷器制作工艺的不断提高，唐朝至元朝年间出现了许多著名的窑口，其中以长沙窑、西村窑、景德镇窑、龙泉窑、建阳窑、吉州窑最为著名。在便捷的交通网络和市舶贸易体制下，广州成为外销瓷器的主要出口港，各大窑口的瓷器大批聚集在此，远销海外。近年来广州城市考古出土的众多窑口瓷器成为该段历史的有力物证。

　　Map of location for Southeast kilns producing exported ceramics in Tang and Song Dynasties. Ceramics has become one of the major exported materials from China since Tang Dynasty onwards. By the time the ceramic making technique was developing constantly, many famous kilns were known from the Tang to the Yuan Dynasty, including Changsha ware, West Village ware, Jingdezhen kiln, Longquan ware, Jianyang ware, Jizhou ware etc. Thanks to the convenient transport and overseas marine trade system, Guangzhou Harbor has become a major harbor for exporting Chinese ceramics from all kinds of kilns, to Japan, Korea, Southeast Asia, India, Arabic Empire, West Asia and Europe. These different wares of ceramics found in Guangzhou in recent years evidence the passing glory in history.

　　长沙窑青釉贴花执壶，唐代。长沙窑位于湖南省长沙市铜官镇瓦渣坪，是唐代南方重要的青瓷窑场。长沙窑瓷器通过广州大量出口到东南亚、西亚等地。

Changsha ware kettle, in spotted celadon glaze, Tang Dynasty. Changsha kiln is from Wazapin, Tongguan town, Changsha city, Hunan province. It was an important porcelain kiln for Qingci wares in South China during the Tang Dynasty. Many Changsha wares had sold to Southeast Asia and West Asia through Guangzhou Harbor.

　　长沙窑青釉褐绿斑壶，唐代。
Changsha ware kettle celadon with greenish brown pattern, Tang Dynasty.

由左至右为唐代长沙窑生产的青釉兽形埙、青釉鸟形埙、褐釉鸟形埙、褐釉壶形埙。
Changsha ware whistles in ram, bird or kettle form, Tang Dynasty.

　　沙边窑出土的陶匣钵，宋代。宋代广州是重要的外贸口岸，本地窑场随之兴盛，番禺区沙边窑即是一例。该窑产品胎呈灰白色，釉色青黄光亮，器物叩击声音清脆。
　　Shabian ware pottery seggar，Song Dynasty. Guangzhou in Song Dynasty (960～1279) was an important harbor for maritime trade, thus bringing up the wake of local ceramic kilns, such as Shabian kiln in Panyu district. Shabian wares is made of gray white clay, in shining blue and yellow graze. Moreover, it sounds beautifully like a jade when one knocks it.

　　宋代广州外销瓷西村窑瓷器。西村窑是北宋时期广州民间外销瓷窑，以青釉瓷为主，黑酱釉为次，还有少量低温绿釉器。器形有凤首壶、军持、罐、盒等29种，受到阿拉伯文化的影响。纹饰以褐色点彩和彩绘为主，周边刻花、盆心绘酱褐色釉菊纹或牡丹的青白釉大盆是西村窑特有的产品。橄榄青釉印团菊和缠枝菊纹的碗、盏、碟、大盆是仿耀州窑产品。西沙群岛和东南亚诸国海域大量出水西村窑瓷器。

West Village Ware was a folk kiln of Guangzhou in the Northern Song Dynasty, mainly in blue graze, sometime in black or brown graze, plus a few green glazes fired in lower temperature. Wares has 29 types, including kettle with phoenix head, kendi, jar, vase, box etc., and heavily influenced by Arabic culture. Its major patterns include brown painting or colored painting. The unique items include a series of big plates in pale blue graze, painted with brown chrysanthemum or peony in center with small floral motifs at the edge. Another series of bowl, plate, dish and huge shallow bowl in olive green graze printed chrysanthemum roundel or bunched chrysanthemum motifs, are copying Yaozhou wares in style. A great number of West Village Ware ceramics are found from the sea near to Western Sand Islands and Southeast Asia.

西村窑青釉彩绘花卉大盘，北宋。菲律宾水域打捞出水。
West Village ware big plate in celadon glaze and colored painted floral motif, Northern Song Dynasty, excavated from the sea of Philippine.

西村窑青釉凤首壶，北宋。香港徐展堂先生捐赠。
West Village ware phoenix head celadon kettle, Northern Song Dynasty, donated by Dr. T. T. Tsui. from Hong Kong.

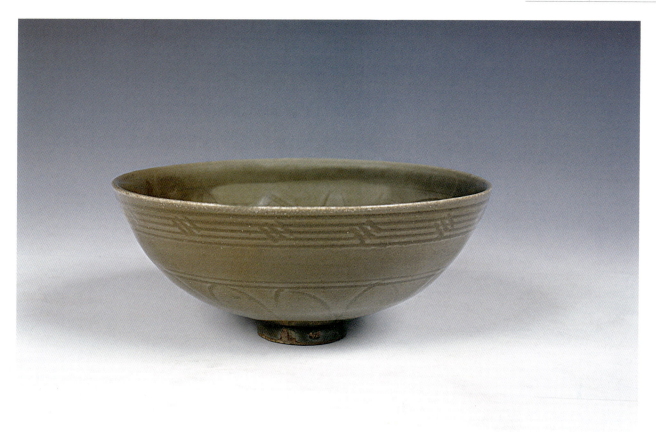

　　龙泉窑青釉刻花瓣纹碗，北宋。龙泉窑位于浙江龙泉，始烧于北宋前期，南宋达到顶峰，生产白胎青瓷的同时，还为南宋宫廷烧造仿官窑的黑胎器物。元代时精于烧制大件器物，除供应全国各地外，大量经广州行销海外，在今日本、南朝鲜、菲律宾、马来西亚、巴基斯坦、印度、埃及等国的古港口及遗址都有龙泉窑瓷器出土。

　　Longquan ware celadon bowl with petal motif, Northern Song Dynasty. Longquan kiln is from Longquan Country, Zhejiang province, first built in the early Northern Song, and reached its peak in the Southern Song Dynasty. Its manufacture included blue grazed white body porcelain, and black porcelain for the Southern Song court. In Yuan Dynasty it was well known for making large wares, for both the domestic market and overseas. Today Longquan wares were found at various sites and harbors in Japan, Korea, Malaysia, Philippine, Pakistan, India, and Egypt etc.

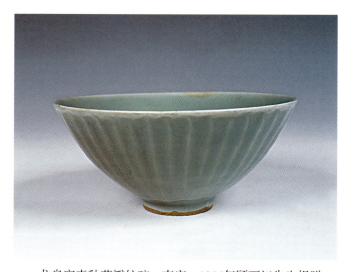

龙泉窑青釉菊瓣纹碗，南宋。1956年顾丽江先生捐赠。

Longquan ware celadon bowl, with chrysanthemum motif, Southern Song Dynasty, donated by Mr. Gu Lijiang in 1956.

龙泉窑青釉印海水龙纹小罐，南宋。

Longquan ware celadon small vase, printed seawater and dragon motif, Southern Song Dynasty.

　　建阳窑兔毫釉盏，宋代。建阳窑是南方著名的黑釉瓷产地，窑址在今福建省建阳县水吉镇，北宋开始烧制，南宋时最盛。以兔毫釉茶盏最为名贵，在黑釉层中透出均匀细密、状若兔毫的自然结晶釉纹样。建阳窑瓷器从广州外销至日本、朝鲜等国，深受当地人青睐。

Jianyang ware bowl in hare fur glaze, Song Dynasty. Jianyang kiln is the famous black graze kiln in the south, situated in Shuiji Town, Jianyang Country, Fujian Province. First appeared in the Northern Song Dynasty, and reached its peak in the Southern Song Dynasty. Among different items the most precious one is the tea bowl in "hare fur glaze", since the thin and fine crystal graze from the black background looks like delicate dare hair. Jianyang ware ceramics are cherished in Korea and Japan, mainly exported from Guangzhou.

　　耀州窑青釉刻花碗，宋代。耀州窑位于今陕西铜川黄堡镇，始烧于唐而终于元。有青釉、白釉、黑釉、酱釉等品种，以刻花、印花装饰为主。北宋刻花青瓷尤精，器物造型有花瓣式、瓜棱式、六折式、多折式，外形美观。河南临汝、宝丰、宜阳和广州西村、广西永福等瓷窑都烧制耀州窑风格的青釉刻花、印花瓷器。

Yaozhou ware celadon bowl with carved pattern, Song Dynasty. Yaozhou kiln is situated in Huangbao Town, Tongchuan Country, Shanxi Province. First appeared in Tang Dynasty and ended in Yuan Dynasty, items include blue graze, white graze, black and brown graze, mainly decorated with carved or printed pattern. The most delicate items are carved pattern in blue graze dated to the Northern Song period, shaped in floriated, or multi-faceted. Yaozhou wares were also produced in Linru, Baofeng, Yiyang country in Henan Province, and the West Village in Guangzhou, Yongfu Country in Guangxi Province, mainly carved or printed pattern in blue graze.

　　吉州窑玳瑁釉花瓣形盏，南宋至元代。吉州窑是宋代著名的民间瓷窑，位于江西吉安市永和镇。最具代表性的是黑釉瓷，伴有木叶纹、玳瑁斑、剪纸贴花、黑釉彩绘、窑变花釉和剔花装饰。南宋至元代是吉州窑产品外销的黄金时期，大批瓷器经广州出口外销。

　　Jizhou ware saucer in turtle shell glaze, shaped in petal, Southern Song to Yuan period. Jizhou kiln is a famous folk kiln in Song Dynasty, situated in Yonghe Town, Ji'an City, Jiangxi Province. The most representative items are in black glaze, decorated with pattern of leaves, turtle shell, paper cutting, appliqué pattern, colored painting on black glaze, along with versatile coloured glaze and openwork carving. Form the Southern Song to Yuan period was the heyday of the Jizhou ware ceramics for exporting abroad via Guangzhou.

吉州窑黑釉盏，宋代。
Jizhou ware plate in black glaze, Song Dynasty.

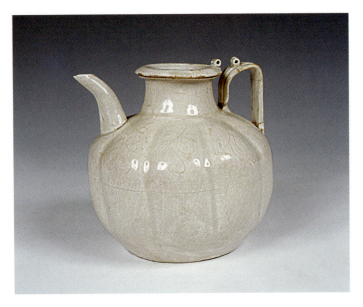

影青瓜棱形执壶，宋代。影青是青白釉瓷的别称，创烧于北宋早期，主要产自景德镇窑，形成以景德镇为中心的南方青白瓷系。宋元时期，江西、福建和广东等地烧造的青白瓷大量外销。近数十年来，在亚洲及非洲沿海地区的古遗址中陆续有青白瓷出土。

Multi-faceted kettle in pale blue glaze, Song Dynasty. "Shadow blue" is a literature name of pale blue glaze, first appeared in the early Northern Song Dynasty, mainly from Jingdezhen kiln and surrounding kilns in South China. In Song and Yuan period, a large scale of ceramics in pale blue glaze made in Jiangxi, Fujian and Guangdong were exported overseas. In recent years, many coast sites in Asia and Africa discovered this type of ceramics in large quantities.

影青杯、托，宋代。1998年5月刘忠山先生捐赠。
Cup and tray in pale blue glaze, Song Dynasty, donated by Mr. Liu Zhongshan in May 1998.

影青贴花双耳瓶，元代。
Vase with two handles in shadow blue glaze with appliqué pattern, Yuan Dynasty.

　　有句谚语"未有羊城，先有光孝"，光孝寺是岭南年代最古老、规模最大的一座名刹，也是中外众多高僧驻锡的佛教道场，是中印佛教文化交流的历史见证物，居岭南佛教丛林之冠。唐代仪凤元年（676年），禅宗六祖惠能在此与寺僧论风幡后削发受戒，开创佛教禅宗南派。

　　It is said locally that "Guangxiao temple exists earlier than the Guangzhou city". Guangxiao monastery was the oldest and biggest temple in Lingnan, in which many Indian and Chinese high monks have stayed, translating sutras and preaching Buddhism. For instance, in 676 AD, the sixth Zen patriarch Huineng joined the famous Zen debate in this temple and then shaved himself to be a monk, who subsequently set up the southern section of the Zen Buddhism in China.

六榕花塔最初为昙裕法师所建木塔，供奉从海外带回的佛舍利，后木塔被焚毁。
Liurong Pagoda was firstly a wooden pagoda built by high monk Tanyu for worshipping Buddha's relics from abroad, but unfortunately the wooden pagoda was burned out later.

鎏金铜佛像，南朝。南北朝时不少佛教僧侣乘商舶来到广州，或从广州出海西行，此佛像是南北朝时期佛教兴旺的佐证。

Bronze Buddha Statue gilded in gold，Southern Dynasties (420～581). During the Southern and Northern Dynasties, many foreign monks on commercial boats from the West arrived Guangzhou to translate sutra and preach Buddhism in China; meanwhile Chinese monks were departing from Guangzhou to India or Southeast Asia to require or obtain sutra. This Buddha statue is the evidence of the prosperity of Buddhism in the Southern and Northern Dynasties.

铁佛像，唐代。1950年广州市光孝寺发现。
Iron statue of Buddha, Tang Dynasty, found in Guangxiao Monastery in Guangzhou in 1950.

木雕力士像，唐代。1950年广州市光孝寺发现。
Wooden statue of Buddhist Heavenly King, Tang Dynasty, found in Guangxiao Monastery in Guangzhou in 1950.

木雕供养人像，唐代。1950年广州市光孝寺发现。
Wooden statue of a Buddhist donor, Tang Dynasty, found in Guangxiao Monastery in Guangzhou in 1950.

木雕罗汉坐像，唐代。1950年广州市光孝寺发现。

Wooden statue of a sitting Arhat, Tang Dynasty, found in Guangxiao Monastery in Guangzhou in 1950.

木雕武士像，唐代。1950年广州市光孝寺发现。

Wooden statue of an armed warrior, Tang Dynasty, found in Guangxiao Monastery in Guangzhou in 1950.

怀圣寺又名狮子寺，俗称光塔寺，是我国现存最古老的清真寺建筑。唐代以来，众多阿拉伯商人定居广州，修建了一座规模宏大的清真寺，即怀圣寺。寺的命名表达了中外教民对圣人穆罕默德的尊从和怀念。

The Huaisheng Mosque is also called Lion Mosque or Light Tower Mosque. It is the oldest muslim mosque in China dated back to the Early Tang. Since Tang Dynasty, thousands of Arabic merchants lived in Guanghzou, in such circumstance a magnificent mosque was built for the local Muslem. It's name "Huaisheng" expressed the follower's respect and forever memory to the founder of Islam Mahomet.

唐代清真先贤古墓位于今广州解放北路桂花岗（兰圃西郊），俗称"回回坟"。

Tombs of Muslim Magus, Tang Dynasty, the so-called "tombs of Huihui" locally, in Guihuagang, Jiefangbei Road, western vicinity of the Orchid Garden, Guangzhou.

光塔位于怀圣寺内，是极具价值的建筑古迹。整个光塔用砖石砌成，最初塔顶有向风飞翔金鸡，多次被飓风吹落后改为葫芦宝顶，晚近改为橄榄形。该塔作为航标，便于海船观察风信。

The minaret "Tower of Light" is situated in the precincts of Huaisheng Mosque, regarded as precious architecture heritage. The minaret is made of bricks and stone slabs. Originally at the top of the minaret there was a pilot cock flying with wind, but was destroyed by turbulent wind many times, so that it was changed to a cucurbit shape and further to a olivary top recently. The minaret was built as a navigation mark to ocean-going vessels.

蒲氏家族墓碑，重刻于清光绪十六年（1891年），记录了阿拉伯人蒲氏家族由宋至明在华生活情况。他们自唐宋入华定居以来，不仅改用汉姓，其后世更经科举晋身仕途，受封为朝廷命官。

Tomb steles of the Pu family, re-carved in 1891 AD, late Qing Dynasty. It records the history of the Arabic living in Guangzhou family from Song to Ming period. Since the family migrated to China in Tang Dynasty, they used Chinese surname "Pu", and some descendents were well educated in Chinese and became civil officials in Chinese court.

　　清代蒲氏宗祠位于广州市珠江村，虽然是典型的珠三角祠堂建筑，但是祠堂内的《蒲氏族谱》证明，该祠是西亚阿拉伯人后裔的宗祠。该蒲氏于明初定居黄埔，娶汉女为妻，至今珠江村内还有两百多名蒲姓后人。该宗祠的发现对研究广州对外贸易和文化交流有重要文物价值。（广州市文物考古研究所提供）

　　This ancestor temple of Pu family is located in Pearl River Village, Guangzhou. It is a typical temple style of Pearl River Delta, but the preserved dictionary of the Pu family tree here records that the Pu family was originally from Arab countries. The Pu family lived in the Pearl River Village, Whampoa, married Chinese girls for generations from early Ming Dynasty. Today there are more than 200 Pu members living in the Pearl River Village. The discovery of the Pu ancestor temple provides a precious case study on the foreign trade and cultural exchange of Guangzhou. (provided by the Cultural Relics and Archaeological Research Institution of Guangzhou)

白釉军持，唐代。军持应是阿拉伯商人定制的，专门为伊斯兰教的穆斯林进行宗教仪式所用。

Kendi in white glaze，Tang Dynasty. Kendi is a kind of water vessel, originated in India and was late specially used by Muslim in Islamic rituals. Kendi made in China were exported mainly for Arabic market.

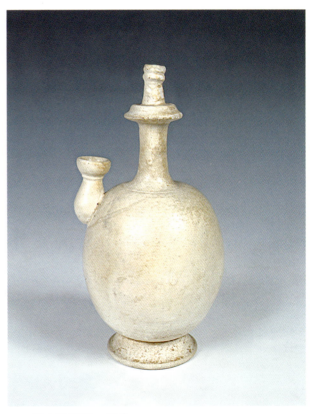

定窑系白釉花口军持，宋代。
Ding Ware kendi in white glaze with petal shaped rim, Song Dynasty.

青白釉军持，元代。
Kendi in pale blue glaze, Yuan Dynasty.

　　黄釉胡人俑，唐代。陶俑的面貌和服饰明显带有唐代西域胡人的特征，深目高鼻，蓄有大束胡子，头戴毡帽，身穿圆领窄袖衣袍。唐代曾有大批胡人经海路或陆路进入中国境内，他们除从事商业、宗教和艺术活动外，亦有少数是宫廷或贵族雇用的奴仆。

　　Ceramic figurines of Sogdian merchants in yellow glaze, Tang Dynasty. These figurines feature in deep-set eyes and aquiline nose, heavy beard, wears fur Phrygian cap and tight-sleeved caftan. A great number of Sogdians arrived China via desert road or via sea, worked as merchants, priests for promoting Zoroastrianism and other foreign religions, musician and artists, as well as servants for the royal families and aristocrats.

宋代胡人俑
Ceramic figurines of Sogdian merchants, Song Dynasty.

高丽穆斯林剌马丹墓碑，元代。碑文记载高丽人剌马丹于元代至正九年（1439年）出任广西陆川县"达鲁花赤"（相当于县令），死于广州。
Tomb stele of Ramadan, the Korean muslim, Yuan Dynasty. It is recorded on the stele that the Korean muslim Ramadan became the mayor of Luchuan Country, Guangxi Province in 1439AD, and late died in Guangzhou.

南汉国都

Hub of the Nanhan Kingdom

公元917年，刘岩称帝广州，建都广州，国号大越，次年改国号汉，史称南汉。宋开宝四年（971年），宋兵入主广州，南汉亡。南汉割据岭南55年，是五代十国时期存在时间较长的一个地方独立王国。南汉国时期，广州对外贸易十分兴盛，岭南地区社会经济得到持续发展。

In 917 AD, by the fall of the Tang Empire, local ruler Liu Yan crowned himself as king of the Nanhan Kingdom in Guangzhou. In 971 AD, the Northern Song army conquered the Nanhan Kingdom and reunited China. As an independent local kingdom, Nanhan lasted for 55 years during the Five Dynasties(907～960AD). During that time, Guangzhou continued its economic development and overseas trade.

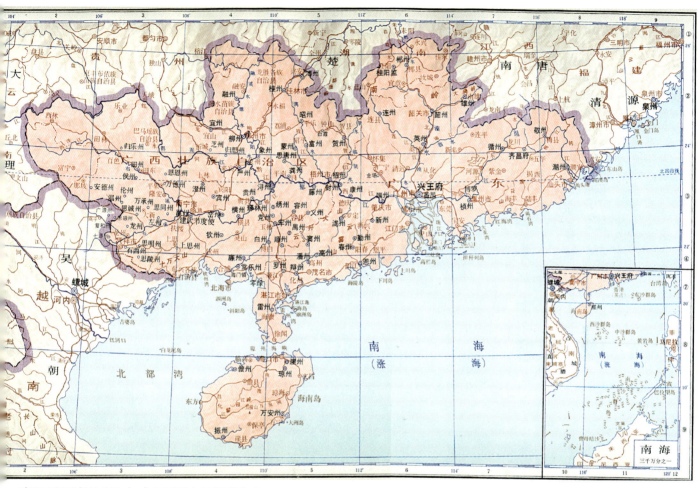

南汉国疆域图（选自《中国历史地图集》）
Map of Territory of the Nanhan Kingdom(917～971)

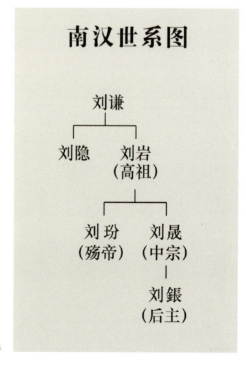

南汉世系图
Royal Family Tree of the Nanhan Kingdom

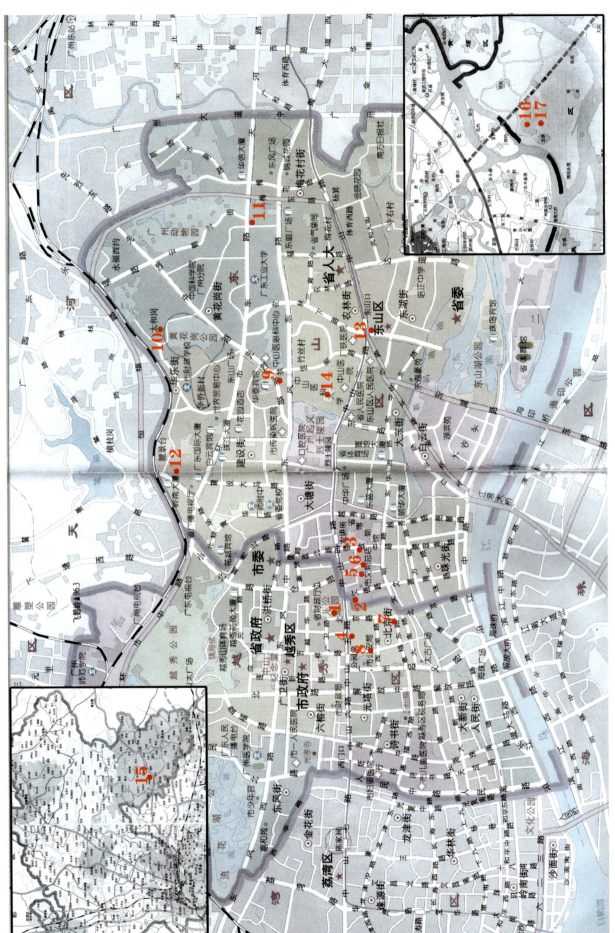

广州已发现的南汉国遗存分布图
Map of location for relics of Nanhan Kingdom in Guangzhou City

左图标示的南汉国遗址说明：

1、南汉宫殿基址，2002年中山四路原儿童公园发掘。

The palace ruins of Nanhan Kingdom, excavated from primary Children Garden, Zhongshansi Road in 2002.

2、南汉建筑基址，2003年中山四路原致美斋地块发掘。

The architecture ruins of Nanhan period, excavated from the Zhimeizhai field, Zhongshansi Road in 2003.

3、南汉水关遗址，1994年德政中路担杆巷南侧发掘。

Water pass site made of wooden structure of Nanhan period, excavated from the south side of Dangan Lane, Dezhengzhong Road in 1994.

4、南汉大型建筑基址，2008年中山五路南、大马站路西侧发掘。

The large scale architecture ruins of Nanhan period, excavated from the south side of Zhongshanwu Road and the west side of Damazhan Road in 2008.

5、南汉宋代城墙遗址，2007年中山四路长塘街西侧发掘。

City wall ruins dated to Nanhan period and Song Dynasty, excavated from the west side of Changtang Street, Zhongshansi Road in 2007.

6、南汉宋代河堤遗址，2008年中山四路大塘街西侧发掘。

Riverbank ruin deted to Nanhan period and Song Dynasty, excavated from the west side of Datang Street, Zhongshansi Road in 2008.

7、南汉道路遗址，2002年北京路发掘。

The ancient road of Nanhan period, excavated from Beijing Road in 2002.

8、南汉药洲遗址，在今教育路。

Herb Islet of Nanhan period, located in Jiaoyu Road.

9、南汉水井遗存，2007年东风东路中山大学肿瘤防治中心工地发掘。

Well ruin dated to Nanhan period, excavated from Tumour Prevention and Cure Center of Zhongshan University, Dongfengdong Road in 2007.

10、南汉墓葬，2008年太和岗发掘。

Tombs of Nanhan period, excavated from Taihegang in 2008.

11、南汉水井与窖藏，2007年环市东路发掘。

Well and cache ruins of Nanhan period, excavated from Huanshidong Road in 2007.

12、南汉建筑遗址，2005年麓湖路发掘。

The architecture ruins of Nanhan period, excavated from Luhu Road in 2005.

13、南汉水井遗存，2006年中山一路东山口发掘。

Well ruin dated to Nanhan period, excavated from Dongshankou, Zhongshanyi Road in 2006.

14、南汉水井遗存，2007年中山二路中山大学医学院内发掘。

Well ruin dated to Nanhan period, excavated from Medical College of Zhongshan University, Zhongshan'er Road in 2007.

15、南汉昭陵（刘晟墓），1954年萝岗区石马村发掘。

Mausoleum of Zhaoling (tomb of the king Liu Cheng) of Nanhan Kingdom, excavated from Shima Villiage, Luogang District in 1954.

16、南汉德陵（刘隐墓），2003年番禺区小谷围岛发掘。

Mausoleum of Deling (tomb of the king Liu Yin) of Nanhan Kingdom, excavated from Xiaoguwei Island, Panyu District in 2003.

17、南汉康陵（刘岩墓），2003年番禺区小谷围岛发掘。

Mausoleum of Kangling (tomb of the king Liu Yan) of Nanhan Kingdom, excavated from Xiaoguwei Island, Panyu District in 2003.

（左图及相关遗址发掘情况由广州市文物考古研究所易西兵提供）

（the map and the excavating materials were provided by Yi Xibing from the Cultural Relics and Archaeological Research Institution of Guangzhou）

南汉康陵陵园，位于番禺小谷围岛北亭村，2003~2004年发掘，是目前已知五代十国陵墓中首次发现的陵园建筑。（广州市文物考古研究所提供）

Mausoleum of Kangling, Nanhan Kingdom, in Beiting Village, Xiaoguwei Island, Panyu. It was excavated from 2003 to 2004，which is the first mausoleum that has been found among tombs dated to Five Dynasties (907~960). (provided by the Cultural Relics and Archaeological Research Institution of Guangzhou)

2003年南汉康陵出土的哀册文碑是目前出土年代最早的哀册文碑石。青灰色石灰岩。首题"高祖天皇大帝哀册文",共1062字。哀册文用成熟的墓志铭文体,在叙述中夹入骈列的赞颂之辞。哀册文称,此墓为南汉高祖刘岩(又名刘龑)的"康陵",刘岩死于大有十五年(942年)四月,同年九月葬于此地。(广州市文物考古研究所提供)

Stone stele of mourning article in Kangling, Nanhan Kingdom, recovered in 2003. It is the earliest stele of mourning article found so far in China. Blue-gray limestone, entitled "Mourning article for the Southern Han emperor Gaozu", carved 1062 words in total. The article uses a mature epitaph style to praise and mourn the late Southern Han emperor Gaozu (named Liu Yan, or Liu Gong). It is recorded on stele that the tomb is called Kangling, while Liu Yan died in April 942 AD, and was buried in September in Kangling. (provided by the Cultural Relics and Archaeological Research Institution of Guangzhou)

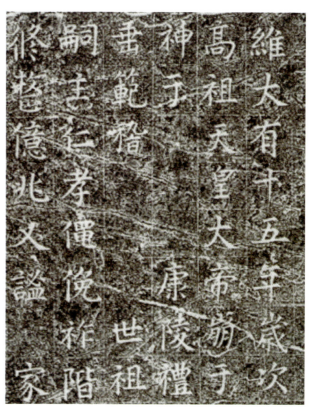

(局部)

陶制岭南佳果象生祭品，2003年南汉康陵出土，均为素胎。分别是香蕉、鸡心柿、菠萝、桃子、荸荠、木瓜、茨菇。这是目前我国发现最早的象生水果。（广州市文物考古研究所提供）

Pottery tropical fruits without glaze, for funerary ceremony, from mausoleum of Kangling, Nanhan Kingdom, excavated in 2003. There are banana, persimmon, pineapple, peach, water chest nut, papaya and water plant arrowhead. These are the earliest fruit models found so far in ancient China. (provided by the Cultural Relics and Archaeological Research Institution of Guangzhou)

玻璃器，2003年南汉康陵出土。呈湖水绿色，较厚处显墨绿色。口沿、肩和底部稍厚，器壁甚薄，上有十一道突棱，为舶来品。（广州市文物考古研究所提供）

Glass ware, form Kangling, Nanhan Kingdom, excavated in 2003. It is mainly in lake green, while its thick part is in dark green. Its mouth, shoulder and bottom are slightly thicker, while the body is thinner, decorated with eleven stripes, which was identified as exotic piece from overseas. (provided by the Cultural Relics and Archaeological Research Institution of Guangzhou)

南汉德陵，位于番禺小谷围岛北亭村，2003～2004年发掘。（广州市文物考古研究所提供）
Mausoleum of Deling, Nanhan Kingdom, in Beiting Village, Xiaoguwei Island, Panyu, excavated from 2003 to 2004. (provided by the Cultural Relics and Archaeological Research Institution of Guangzhou)

　　南汉青瓷盖罐。2003年南汉德陵墓道南端器物箱里出土青釉罐190件，釉陶罐82件。这批青釉罐为五代时期青瓷珍品。（广州市文物考古研究所提供）

In 2003 at the south end of the tomb corridor of mausoleum Deling, Nanhan Kingdom, 190 pieces of ceramic vases in blue graze and 82 pottery vase in coloured graze were found. These ceramic vases in blue graze are regarded as the valuable articles among ceramic dated to the Five Dynasties(907～960). (provided by the Cultural Relics and Archaeological Research Institution of Guangzhou)

　　越窑"官"字款青瓷盘底，南汉。青釉表面有玻璃光泽，并有细密冰裂纹片。（广州市文物考古研究所提供）

Yue ware plate in blue graze, marked with "guan" (meaning for royal use) at the bottom, dated to Nanhan period. The blue graze is as shinning as glass, with thin and fine ice-crashing motif.(provided by the Cultural Relics and Archaeological Research Institution of Guangzhou)

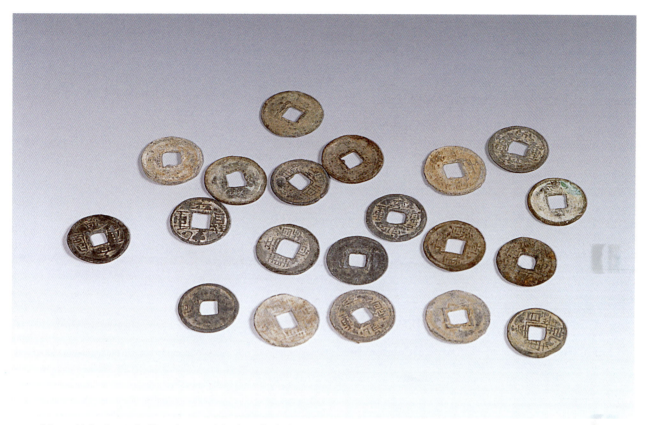

南汉"乾亨重宝"铅钱。南汉国为解决通货膨胀问题，大量铸造铅钱。

Lead coin of "Qianheng zhong bao" dated to Nanhan period. A large quantity of lead coins were moulded in the Nanhan kingdom, in order to solve the inflation problem.

　　南汉政权在广州大造宫苑。考古发掘证实，宫殿区在今中山四路原儿童公园所在地。图为1997年发掘的宫殿区石山莲池（上图）和2000年发掘的体形巨大的南汉殿堂磉墩遗址（下图）。2002年发掘了宫殿石板地面，2003年南汉大型建筑群落遗存呈现于世人面前。（广州市文物考古研究所提供）

　　A great series of palace was built by the Nanhan court in Guangzhou. Archaeological excavations show that the palace was located originally at the Children's Park, Zhongshansi Road. In 1997 the royal lotus pond and stone hill were discovered, both of which originally belonged to the Nanhan palace; and in 2002 the stone floor of the palace was unearthed; furthermore, in 2003 a large scale of palace ruins were excavated. (provided by the Cultural Relics and Archaeological Research Institution of Guangzhou)

　　南汉宫殿内特大型石柱础，2000年广州中山四路发掘。柱础上雕刻16只狮子，雌雄各半，造型十分独特，应受外来文明影响所致。（广州市文物考古研究所提供）

　　The huge stone pillar base of the Nanhan palace, discovered in 2000 from Zhongshansi Road. Sixteen lions are depicted on the pillar, eight female and eight male, in a unique western style. (provided by the Cultural Relics and Archaeological Research Institution of Guangzhou)

　　陶脊兽，南汉。2003年中山四路致美斋工地出土。造型独特。龙头形，长鼻如象拔，上卷，向外张嘴露牙。内侧作套筒，弧顶平底。外侧面塑獠牙、圆目。套筒弧顶近鼻处有两个圆形钉孔，以安置固定插件。（广州市文物考古研究所提供）

　　Pottery mythical animal, roof ornam zzent, dated to Nanhan period, unearthed from the Zhimeizhai field, Zhongshansi Road in 2003. The mythical animal, perhaps Makara, has a dragon head, with a long elephant trunk curling up, and opening month with fearsome tusks. The inner part is a cylinder with an arch top, while the outer part depicts a monster with staring eyes and threatening tusks. Near to the arch top, two round holes at the nose were originally for fixing round headed nails and padding things. (provided by the Cultural Relics and Archaeological Research Institution of Guangzhou)

脊瓦饰，南汉。2003年中山四路致美斋工地出土。筒瓦末端附加泥塑兽头，塑出龇牙咧嘴之态，为戗脊上的走兽。（广州市文物考古研究所提供）

Pottery roof tile shaped in mythical animal，roof ornament, dated to Nanhan period, unearthed from the Zhimeizhai field, Zhongshansi Road in 2003. A mythical animal with tusks in clay is depicted at the end of the tube roof tile, supposedly to be the ornament object at the axis of the roof spine. (provided by the Cultural Relics and Archaeological Research Institution of Guangzhou)

鬼面瓦，南汉。兽面，额上双角相牴，下为高鼻圆目，龇牙咧嘴，长舌卷曲下垂，下部刻划鬃须，面目狰狞。额上中间有一圆形钉孔，以安置固定插件。（广州市文物考古研究所提供）

Eave tile in shape of monster, Nanhan period. The monster has a fearsome animal face, with two horns confronted each other on forehead, shaped nose and staring eyes, opening mouth and irritating teeth, with long tongue stretched downwards, and heavy beard. A round hole is made on the forehead to fix the padding instrument.(provided by the Cultural Relics and Archaeological Research Institution of Guangzhou)

青釉滴水瓦，南汉。（广州市文物考古研究所提供）
Tile of dropping water in blue glaze, Nanhan period. (provided by the Cultural Relics and Archaeological Research Institution of Guangzhou)

黄釉双凤纹瓦当，南汉。（广州市文物考古研究所提供）
Eave tile in yellow glaze, decorated with confronted phoenixes, Nanhan period. (provided by the Cultural Relics and Archaeological Research Institution of Guangzhou)

绿釉瓦当，南汉。（广州市文物考古研究所提供）
Eave tile in green glaze, Nanhan period. (provided by the Cultural Relics and Archaeological Research Institution of Guangzhou)

莲花瓦当，南汉。（广州市文物考古研究所提供）
Eave tile decorated with lotus motif, Nanhan period. (provided by the Cultural Relics and Archaeological Research Institution of Guangzhou)

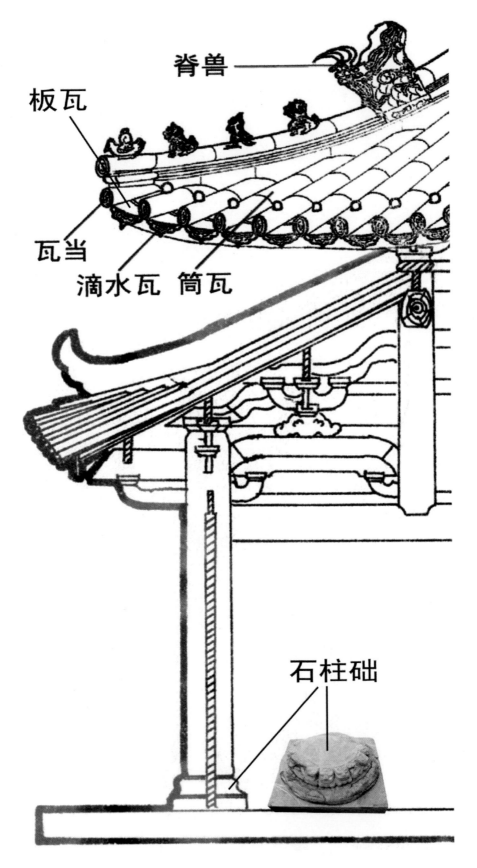

脊兽

板瓦

瓦当

滴水瓦　筒瓦

石柱础

建筑构件示意图
Line Drawing: Functions of some kinds of architectural components

　　黄釉莲花纹铺地砖，南汉。2003年中山四路致美斋工地出土。砖心为莲蓬，其外为复瓣莲花，四角各饰一朵折枝菊花纹，做工精美。（广州市文物考古研究所提供）

　　Floor bricks in yellow glaze, decorated in lotus motif, Nanhan period, unearthed from the Zhimeizhai field, Zhongshansi Road in 2003. It delicately depicts a lotus seedpod in center surrounded by a thousand petals lotus, along with a twig of chrysanthemum at each corner. (provided by the Cultural Relics and Archaeological Research Institution of Guangzhou)

　　南汉皇家园林药洲遗址。南汉乾亨三年(919年)，刘岩在今广州西湖路、教育路一带，利用原来的天然池沼凿长湖五百丈(约1600米)，史称西湖或仙湖。湖中建洲炼丹求仙药，故称药洲。湖中有瑰奇怪石九块，美称九曜石。沿湖有亭、楼、馆、榭，风景甚美。

　　Site of the Herb Islet, in the royal park of the Nanhan Kingdom. In 919 AD, King of Nanhan built a long lake, the so-called "West Lake" or "Immortal Lake" in history. The lake was 1600 m in length, on the base of the nature pool around the West Lake Road. The Herb Islet was built in the middle of the lake, for making immortal medicine for the king. Nine beautiful stones stand in the lake in an order, which was named "Stone of Nine Stars". Along the lake bank there were pavilions, towers, inns and balconies, famous for the beautiful scenery.

南汉宫苑芳华苑内使用的铁花盆
Iron flower container used in Royal Botanic Garden of Nanhan Kingdom

　　南汉水关遗址，位于广州德政中路唐代木构基址的西侧。水关，即城墙下的排水涵洞，可以起到排污防盗的作用，是南汉时期一处重要的城市排水遗址。（广州市文物考古研究所提供）

Water pass site made of wooden structure, Nanhan period, is located at the west wing of the Tang wooden building, at Dezhengzhong Road, Guangzhou. Water pass is the water channel underneath the city wall, for releasing daily used water and avoiding flood. It was an important achievement on city building during the Nanhan period in Guangzhou.(provided by the Cultural Relics and Archaeological Research Institution of Guangzhou)

　　南汉铁塔，位于今光孝寺内。铁塔的铸造，既表明南汉政权崇佛，也表明南汉的炼铁业和铸造业发达。
　　The Nanhan Iron Pagoda in the Guangxiao monastery. It shows the warm Buddhist believe of the Nanhan court, and the contemporary superior technique of the iron making.

三城合一
Three Towns in One City

唐代广州已形成了牙城、子城和罗城"三重"格局。南汉时又将兴王府广州城规划为宫城、皇城和郭城。宋代是广州城市建设的重要时期。宋熙宁元年（1068年）在子城东扩筑东城，五年后，为保护新兴西部商业区和外商聚居地，又扩筑了西城，形成了"三城"格局。明代洪武十三年（1380年），永嘉侯朱亮祖修建广州城，合宋元三城为一城，并向北扩展，加筑外城；清代又增修东、西翼城，拓至珠江边，形成了今广州老城区的格局。

Since Tang Dynasty Guangzhou city had developed three towns , including Yacheng, Zicheng and Luocheng. During the Nanhan period, the great Guangzhou city was well planed to have the Palace Town, the Royal Town and the Commercial Town in one city wall. In 1068 AD , at the east side of the Zicheng the Eastern Town was built; five years later, in order to protect the rising western commercial district and the dwelling region for foreign merchants, the Western Town was built, thus three towns were linked in one. In 1380 AD (Early Ming Dynasty), Marquis Zhu Liangzu rebuilt Guangzhou city and united the three old towns into one, which further covered the northern vicinity, added with the surrounding outer-city. In Qing Dynasty, two towns at the eastern wing and western wing were built，thus the city was enlarged up to the Pearl River bank. It was the core of the modern Guangzhou city today.

广州德政中路出土的唐、南汉、宋代三叠城。
City ruins through Tang, Nanhan and Song Dynasties, discovered at Dezhengzhong Road.

越秀北路东濠涌截污工程发现的宋代城墙。
City wall ruins dated to Song Dynasty, discovered at Yuexiubei Road.

　　唐代《宋璟碑》记载，唐代广州城以茅草屋为主。而考古证明，唐代广州城市建设达到了较高水平，建筑构件精致，图案精美。这是考古出土南汉宫殿中的莲瓣纹瓦当。

Roof tile shaped in lotus petal, discovered from Nanhan palace.

鬼面瓦，唐代。广州市中山四路出土。
Roof tile with Monster motif, Tang Dynasty. Discovered at zhongshansi Road.

鬼面壁饰，唐代。广州市中山四路出土。
Wall ornament with monster motif, Tang Dynasty. Discovered at zhongshansi Road.

莲花瓦当，唐代建筑构件。
Eave tile with lotus motif, Tang architecture pieces.

宋代广州主要修城活动表
CHRONOLOGICAL TABLE OF BUILDING GUANGZHOU CITY DURING THE SONG DYNASTY

年代	修城工程
景祐四年（1037）	修补城要处。
庆历四年（1044）	经略使魏瓘修筑子城。
皇祐四年（1052）	修筑东、西、南子城瓮城。
熙宁初年（1068）	吕居简请转运使王靖修筑东城。王靖在城外挖壕环城，在城东、南、北三面依次开震东、迎薰、拱辰三门。熙宁四年（1071）程师孟筑西城，保护城西居民。
元丰二年（1079）	浚城壕。
元丰三年（1080）	修城垒。
绍兴元年（1094）	修补城墙。
绍兴二十二年（1152）	修补三城。
嘉泰元年（1201）	修补城墙。
嘉定三年（1210）	陈岘在州城东南、西南隔筑西翅城，保护城南的居民，谓之雁翅城，并维修旧有的城楼。绍定二年（1229）方大琮在广州城旧址创建团楼、炮台，并修葺城门、城墙。
绍定三年（1230）	修补城墙。
绍定六年（1233）	增修三城城墙。
端平年间（1234-1236）	彭铉修葺外城、子城和瓮城。
淳祐二年（1242）	摧锋军修城。
宝祐二年（1254）	摧锋军修城。
开庆元年（1259）	经略使谢子强大修城堡，把城壕扩宽至二十丈，深三丈。
开庆二年（1260）	勇敢军修城。
景定元年（1260）	水军、勇敢军等修城。
景定二年（1261）	预备军修城。

　　宋代广州主要修城活动表。在广州古代城市建设史上，宋代是一个辉煌时期。宋代对广州城进行扩建和修筑达20多次，最重要的工程是新筑子城、东城和西城，史称宋代三城。子城为官衙所在，东城为商业区，西城为蕃汉杂居地，珠江沿岸形成沿江商业区。此格局一直延续到明清。

Chronological table of building Guangzhou City, during the Song Dynasty. Song Dynasty was a significant period for the architecture history of the ancient Guangzhou city. More than 20 times of enlargement and rebuilding works had done to the city, among them the most decisive project were newly building the Zicheng, Eastern Wing Town and Western Wing Town, the so-called "three towns of Song Dynasty". The Zicheng was the place for governing offices, and the Eastern Wing Town was a marketing region, while the Western Wing Town was dowelling area for foreign merchants and envoys. The large scale of bazzar was established along the Pearl River bank up to Ming and Qing Dynasties.

宋代"水军广州修城"戳印砖，表明广州水军有烧造修城砖。
City wall brick with the stamp of " Guangzhou city wall rebuilt by navy", Song Dynasty. From this we learn that the Guangzhou navy was involved in the city-rebuilding project.

宋代嘉泰元年（1201年）修城砖。
City wall brick with the stamp of "city wall rebuilt in the first year of Jiatai Reign", dated to 1201 AD, Song Dynasty.

南宋端平三年（1236年）摧锋军广州修城砖。
City wall brick with the stamp of "Guangzhou city wall rebuilt by Cuifeng Army in the third year of Duanping Reign", dated to 1236 AD, Song Dynasty.

宋代景定元年（1260年）修城砖，上刻"景定元年造御备砖勇敢黎"，表明这是一位黎姓厢兵烧造的。
City wall brick inscribed by "city wall rebuilt by soldier Lee in the first year of Jingding Reign", dated to 1260 AD, Song Dynasty.

宋代广州三城自来水装置模

　　宋代广州城模型，清晰呈现了宋代广州三城的格局，以及利用竹制管道从白云山引水入城的自来水系统。近年来，城市考古相继发现了宋代东城和子城的城墙遗迹，北京路宋代古道路、门楼遗迹的发现，形象地展示了宋代广州城市风貌。

Model of Guangzhou city in Song Dynasty. In recent years, excavations in Guangzhou city proper revealed the city wall ruins of the Eastern Town and Central Town in Song Dynasty. Besides, traces of the ancient road and the ruin of the city gate pavilion at Beijing Road were found, both dated to the Song Dynasty. These materials give us vividly an impression of the City Guangzhou during Song period.

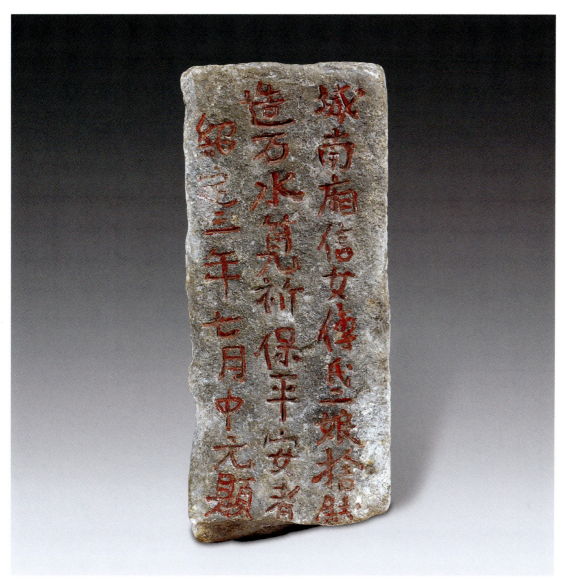

　　三国东吴时，广州刺史陆胤修建引水工程，引白云山泉水入城，解决了城内居民饮水问题。白云山泉水清凉甘甜，故名"甘溪"。甘溪泉水经上塘、下塘，在小北花圈附近分流两支：一支经今仓边路入清水濠，另一支经今大石街华宁里入今西湖路的"古西湖"。宋代甘溪因水源不足而渐渐干涸。北宋时官府引流和疏导甘溪，使其除饮用外，还负有载船运货、排水泄水和灌溉农田的作用。这是宋代广州城市建设的另一重大成果。此外，还修筑六脉渠，疏浚西澳和东澳，深挖四大濠，大规模开发、整治城市用水和排水系统。

　　这是南宋石水笕题刻。石水笕是石制的引水管道。古代广州秋冬季节雨水较少，珠江又受海潮倒灌影响而咸苦，城中居民缺少淡水。北宋苏东坡曾建议用竹管引白云山泉水入城。这是南宋绍定三年（1230年）用石制引水管道引水入城的物证。

In the Three Kingdom Period (220 ~ 265AD), Guangzhou Mayor Lu Ying built water channel from the Baiyun Mountain to the city, therefore benefiting the city people to drink creek water from the hill. The creek water is cold and sweet, called as "Ganxi" (Sweet Creek) locally. The creek runs through Shangtang and Xiatang, and divided into two bracnches at Xiaobeihuaquan, one runs via Cangbian Road to Qingshui Hao; the other runs via the Big Stone Lane to the ancient West Lake. However, from time to time the Ganxi Creek dried out. In the Northern Song Dynasty, the government took out mud and rebuilt water channels, not only for citizen daily drinking, but also for shipping commodity, releasing water and irrigating farms. It was a great achievement of Guangzhou city in Song Dynasty. Besides, Six cannels were built, west and east creek were cleaned, four water irrigation conduits were deeply dug, thus the city drinking and releasing water systems were established.

　　This is the inscription carved on the stone conduit. Because in autumn and winter ancient Guangzhou hardly had rains, and the sea tide goes into the Pearl River, made the fresh water became salty and bitter, city people were suffered from lacking of drinking water. In the Northern Song Dynasty Mayor Su suggested guiding the creek from the Baiyun Mountain into city by using bamboo tubes. The picture testify to the fact that in 1230AD (Southern Song Dynasty) Guangzhou people used stone conduits to receive hill creek from suburban.

　　六脉渠始建于宋代，明清两朝多次疏通。六条排水大渠构成广州城的地下排水道，水流经六脉渠流到东、西濠涌，再进入玉带河，最后归入大海，起到分洪、排水、蓄洪、蓄潮、防旱涝的作用。现在六脉渠和玉带河、西濠已改作暗渠，仍是广州市区重要的排水渠道。此为清代"重浚广东省城六脉渠碑"局部。

　　The Six Cannels was firstly built in Song Dynasty and recleaned several time in Ming and Qing Dynasties. It functions as leasing used water from the city underground, running through east and west creek，into Jade Belt River and eventually approaching the South China Sea. It could protect the city from the flood and dryness and stormy sea tide. Today the Six Cannels and the Jade Belt River and the West creek become underground cannels, but are still used by the modern city as a major water-releasing system. Here is a part of drawiny on a tablt "rebuild the six-vein canal in the capital of Guangdong province" dated to Qing Dynasty.

"左卫前所"红砂岩石，明代。1996年中山五路明代六脉渠遗址出土。明代洪武十三年改都尉为五卫（中、前、后、左、右），卫下辖千户所。京都以外的卫所直属地方都督府管辖，表明卫所参与修筑六脉渠。（广州市文物考古研究所提供）

Reddish Rock，inscribed by "front bureau of the left wei"，Ming Dynasty. Excavated from the site of the Six Cannels at Zhongshan Road in 1996. In early Ming, the royal army changed its name to five army (including the middle, front, behind, left and right), each army in charged of thousands of families. Except from the capital Beijing, all the army were under the supervision of local city government.(provided by the Cultural Relics and Archaeological Research Institution of Guangzhou)

2004年大通寺遗址出土了多件北宋青瓷碗，其中多个碗底有"大通"二字的墨书铭记，这为确认"大通烟雨"井提供了重要物证。（广州市文物考古研究所提供）

In 2004 from the site of Datong monastery a group of ceramic bowls in blue graze dated to the Northern Song were recovered，among them some painted inscription of "Datong" in ink at the bottom of the bowl, which proves that the precise location of the ruined monastery.(provided by the Cultural Relics and Archaeological Research Institution of Guangzhou)

2004年考古工作者重新清理的"大通烟雨井"遗址。史书记载，烟雨井在大通寺里，晨曦初散，井口飘起缕缕轻烟，故有"大通烟雨井"之美名。"大通烟雨井"在宋、元两朝均被列为羊城八景。（广州市文物考古研究所提供）

In 2004 archaeologists excavated the ruin of the Well of Datong. According to historic source, the well in Datong monastery used to have smoke and drizzle in dawn, regarded as one of the eight special scenery of Guangzhou in Song and Yuan Dynasties. (provided by the Cultural Relics and Archaeological Research Institution of Guangzhou)

（日天壶壶身铭文拓片）

　　元代铜壶滴漏，是我国现存最大、最完整的古代计时器。元代延祐三年（1316年），广州冶铸工人冼运行等人铸造，由四个大小不等的铜壶组成，依次安放在阶梯式的座架上，通高2.64米。置于最上的是"日天壶"，其次为"夜天壶"，第三是"平水壶"，最下的是"受水壶"，各壶皆有盖。第一、二、三壶下端装有滴水龙头，依次滴入受水壶，受水壶中央插铜尺一把，尺上刻有十二时辰，自下而上为子至亥时。铜尺前插放一木制浮箭，下为浮舟，随着水位提高，浮箭逐渐上升，显示时间，故又称"刻漏"。在第三壶的壶盖上还安放一兽型器物，用来镇邪。铜壶滴漏原放在广州古城拱北楼上（今北京路），为全城报时。1919年广州拆城开马路时移置越秀山镇海楼。

Bronze water-dropping clock, dated to Yuan Dynasty. It is the biggest and best preserved water-dropping clock in ancient China. In 1316 AD, mounded by the blacksmith studio of Xian Yunxing in Guangzhou. It is 2.64 m in height, made of four bronze bottles from small into large size, putting on four stair bases one by one. From the top to the bottom, they are called respectively "Bottle of the Sun", "Bottle of the Night", "Bottle of floating water", "Bottle of receiving water", all of which have lids. The three high bottles drop water through plumbers, one by one, into the lowest one. At the lowest bottle there is a bronze ruler in the middle marked with 12 hours from the midnight to the noon. In front of the bronze ruler, there is a wooden floating arrow, underneath is a floating boat. By the time the water level is higher and higher, so that the floating arrow is going up and up to show the special hour, which is called "Carved Drops". On the lid of the third bottle, some mythical animals are depicted for driving away evil spirits. This water-dropping clock was originally situated at the Gongbeilou of the ancient Guangzhou City, clocking daily for the whole city. It was moved to the Zhenhai Tower atop of Yuexiu Mountain in 1919 when the city wall and city gate were abandoned and the modern street was built.

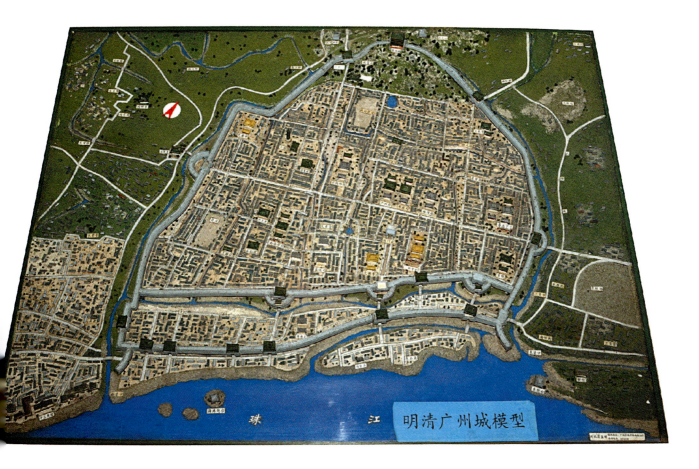

明代洪武十三年（1380年），永嘉侯朱亮祖修建广州城，合宋元三城为一城，向北扩展，并加筑外城；清代在此基础上增修东、西翼城，拓至珠江边，形成"东村西俏南富北贫"的格局。从此，广州城垣臻于完备，直至1918年广州拆城墙、筑马路。这是明清广州城模型。

In 1380 AD (Early Ming Dynasty), Marquis Zhu Liangzu rebuilt Guangzhou city and united the three old towns into one, which further covered the northern vicinity, added with the surrounding outer-city. In Qing Dynasty, based on the Ming city, two towns at the eastern wing and western wing were built, thus the city was enlarged up to the Pearl River bank. In a folk song Guangzhou city in Qing time was described as " The wealth all in the southern town, the poors tightly in the northern town, villages in the eastern wing, while beauties in the western wing." The city was functioning completely since then. In 1918, the ancient city wall was abandoned and modern roads were built for cars and buses. Here is the city model of Guangzhou in Ming and Qing period.

清代广州城坊图
Drawing of the city blocks of Guangzhou in Qing Dynasty

清末越秀山城墙及镇海楼
City wall along the Yuexiu Mountain and the Zhenhai Tower in late Qing Dynasty

越秀山上一千余米长的明清城墙，为广州现仅存的一段城墙遗址。
The ancient city wall atop of the Yuexiu Mountain, around 1000m in length, dated to Ming and Qing Dynasties, is the only preserved city wall of Guangzhou until today.

　　1380年朱亮祖向北扩展广州城时，在越秀山顶修建了一座五层楼以壮观瞻，取名"镇海"，以示"威镇岭海"之意。镇海楼与越秀山古城墙连成一片，是明清时期重要的城市防御设施，也是广州古城重要的标志性建筑。

　　In 1380 when Marquis Zhu enlarged the Guangzhou city to the north, he built a five-story pavilion at the top of the Yuexiu Mountain, named "Zhenhai", meaning "calming down the sea". The pavilion linked with the ancient city wall along the Yuexiu Mountain, was an important citadel during Ming and Qing Dynasties, also a representative building of old Guangzhou.

帝 国 商 行
Co-hong of Imperial China

　　从明朝中叶开始，广州逐渐卷入了国际贸易体系中。随着国内外贸易的繁荣，清政府在广州开设十三行，以行商垄断外贸。广州被指定为全国唯一对外通商口岸后，客观上促使了广州成为国际贸易中心和大清帝国的南风窗。十三行在广州历史发展和中西文化交流中扮演了十分重要的角色。

Since the middle Ming Dynasty, Guangzhou had performed actively in the world trading system. With the trade between foreign ships and Chinese merchants flourishing, the Qing court set up Guangzhou Co-hong (shisan hang) with authorized Hong merchants to monopolize the trade, thus to establish Guangzhou as an international trading centre as well as a window of the southern Qing Empire. Guangzhou was the only port chosen by the Qing court to handle trading activities with foreign merchants. The Co-hong played a key role in the evolution of Guangzhou and the cultural exchange between the West and the East.

明代铁锚。广州制造。四爪，通高3.4米，是广州目前发现最大的古代铁锚。1978年六榕路铁局巷出土。

Iron anchor. Ming Dynasty, made in Guangzhou, with four crows, in total 3.4m in height. It is the biggest ancient iron anchor found in Guangzhou according to present knowledge. Uncovered from Tiejuxiang, Liurong Road in 1978.

却金亭碑记。明嘉靖年间，番禺知县李恺简化商舶入口制度并谢绝外商赠金，暹罗（今泰国）商人筹建却金亭致意。这块碑文反映了明嘉靖年间广州对外贸易的繁盛。

Stone stek of *Que Jin Ting*. In the Jiajing reign of the Ming Dynasty, Magistrate of Panyu county, Li Kai, simplified the custom clearance procedures for foreign boats and declined the reward from foreign merchants. Therefore, the Siamese (now Thai) merchants had the Que Jin Ting (literally Reward Decline Pavilion) constructed in honour of Li Kai. This incident shows the thriving trade in Guangzhou during the Jiajing reign.

　　李凤石像。李凤，明万历二十七至四十二年（1599～1614年）把持广东市舶司的太监，征敛财富，贪酷残暴，严重干预和破坏市舶司的职责和正常运作。

Stone figure of Li Feng. Li Feng, a corrupt eunuch in charge of the Canton Custom House from the 27th year to the 42nd year of the Wanli Reign (1599～1614), Ming Dynasty, misused his authority by meddling in the management of the Custom House.

　　中国海船出海时一般携带火炮，以防海盗。这是清代海船铜炮。

Chinese ships were normally equipped with cannons in case they confronted pirates. This is a bronze cannon made for ships in the Qing Dynasty.

　　黄埔锚地，约1810年，象牙油画。自1685年清廷开放海禁，至1757年广州一口通商，欧美各国到中国贸易的商船约有百分之九十经黄埔港入广州，黄埔港成为外国商船来华丈量吨位、缴纳关税和卸货的地方。黄埔成为广州最繁忙的港口。

　　Whampoa anchorage, C.1810, oil on ivory. From 1685 when the Qing court lifted the sea-trade ban to 1757 when Guangzhou was decreed the only trading port, 90% of merchant ships from Europe and America entered Guangzhou through the whampoa port. As the merchant ships had to have their tonnage measured, duties paid, and cargo unloaded in the whampoa port, the Port became the busiest port in Guangzhou.

　　黄埔地形图，1913年，纸质，铅印，广东陆军测量局制。
　　The Relief Map of whampoa Port, paper, letterpress printing in 1913, drawn by the Bureau of Surveying and Mapping of Land Forces in Canton.

清代广州富商私家花园
A private garden owned by an affluent Chinese merchant in Guangzhou in the Qing Dynasty.

（正面）

（侧面）

（背面）

"十三行怡心馆" 木箱，邹伯奇后人邹孟才捐。
A wooden box with the mark of Yi Xin Firm from 13 Hongs, donated by Zou Mengcai, Zou Boqi's descendant.

石湾窑洋人抱瓶立像，清末。洋人头戴礼帽，深目高鼻，肩系披风，脚穿长筒靴，右足踏松毛狗，将欧洲商人的形象表现得淋漓尽致。

Figurine of a Foreigner holding a vase, produced by the Shiwan kiln at the end of the Qing Dynasty. The foreigner, with a hat on head, a cloak around shoulder and boots on feet, has sunken eyes and a high nose, sculpted incisively and vividly, he places his right foot on a Chow Chow.

　　广州十三行商馆，18世纪末19世纪初，玻璃画。十三行商馆是清政府唯一允许外商居住和贸易的地方，简称"商馆"，又名"夷馆"，是十三行行商为租赁给外商而专门兴建的。货船从珠江上载运货物进来，停靠在粤海关设立的"船屋"，经过粤海关的检查，即可到商馆卸货。商馆既是货栈，又是宿舍、店铺，食宿、做账、谈价、验货、发货、娱乐、祷告等，均在此进行。外商在此出售呢绒、棉布、钟表等"洋货"，购回中国的茶叶、瓷器、丝织品等。

Canton Foreign Factories, from the end of the 18th century to early of the 19th century, glass painting. The commercial factories of the 13 Hongs were the only place permitted by the Qing court for foreign merchants to live and trade; these factories in Chinese were also called *shang guan* or *yi guan*, which the Hong merchants had constructed to be let to foreign merchants. The loaded ship that came along the Pearl River would stopp over the "ship house" that was run by Canton Custom House to receive an inspection by Chinese custom officers, before it was unloaded at the commercial hall. A commercial hall functioned as a dormitory, a store, and an eating place, where foreign merchants could keep accounts, negotiate the prices, inspect the goods, deliver the goods, have fun and say a prayer, etc. Right at the commerc factories, goods such as woollen cloth, cotton cloth, clocks and watches, were traded for Chinese treasures: tea, porcelain and silk textiles.

称茶，约19世纪，通草水彩画。茶叶是18、19世纪中西贸易最重要的物品。清代广州是中国最大的茶叶市场，粤海关每年征收的茶税约四十万两。荷兰东印度公司早于1606年至1607年从澳门贩运中国茶叶至巴达维亚（今印尼雅加达），约于1610年转运至欧洲，欧洲人对茶叶嗜爱有加。从18世纪起，欧洲掀起了一股"中国热"，饮茶更是成为欧洲人的一种生活习尚，与茶有关的文化深刻地影响着欧洲人的生活方式。据统计，当时英国每年平均以十分之一的收入用来购买中国茶叶。

Weighting tea in Guangzhou, about 19th century, watercolour painting on pith. Tea was deemed the most important goods in the Sino-West trade of the 18th and 19th century. Guangzhou in the Qing Dynasty was the largest tea market, which provided a yearly taxation of 400,000 taels of silver to Canton Custom House. Early in 1606 and 1607, the Dutch East Indian Company already shipped Chinese tea to Batavia（now Jakarta, the capital of Indonesia）, where it was further transferred to Europe from 1610. The Europeans loved Chinese tea so much that from the 18th century on, yumcha became a fashion among Europeans and tea culture had a deep impact on their life style. Statistically speaking, ten percent of British income paid for Chinese tea at that time.

广州同孚行茶叶外销，约19世纪，通草水彩画。
Tong Fu Firm exported tea from Guangzhou, about 19th century, watercolour painting on pith.

　　"哥德堡号"船模，瑞典西方古董公司捐赠。"哥德堡"号是一艘以瑞典东印度公司总部所在城市哥德堡命名的重要船只，为瑞典东印度公司所有船只中的第二大船只。船长82米，排水量约为833吨，船上装备有30门大炮，约有140名船员。1739～1745年间该船曾三次远航广州，其中第三次航行装载了包括100吨瓷器在内的700吨中国货物，1745年9月12日在距哥德堡口岸约900米远的海域触礁沉没。从出水瓷器看，"哥德堡"号装载的主要是青花瓷，约占所购瓷器的四分之三。

　　Ship model of Götheburg, donated by the Antique West company in Sweden. It was the second biggest ocean-going commercial vessel belonged to the Sweden Eastern Indian Company, named after the local city Götheburg. It was 82m in length, of 833 tons displacement, equipped with 30 cannons and 140 sailors. From 1739 to 1745 it travelled to Guangzhou for three times. On its third journey it contained 700 tons of commodities from China, including 100 tons of porcelain, but unfortunately was sank down within coral reefs only 900m far to the Götheburg harbour on 12th of September, 1745. According to the salvaged porcelain in recent years, around three quarters of the Chinese porcelain were blue and white wares.

瑞典"哥德堡号"商船出水的福建白毫茶。
Fukien pekoe found from the Swedish shipwreck Götheborg.

瑞典"哥德堡号"商船出水的福建白毫茶，至今色味仍存。（由中山大学蔡鸿生教授提供）
Fukien pekoe found from the Swedish shipwreck Götheborg still keeps its colour and flavour. (The pekoe was provided by Prof. Cai Hongsheng of Sun Yat-Sen University)

　　瑞典"哥德堡号"沉船打捞出水的青花瓷片，分别为2002年10月瑞典访问中国代表团赠送给广州市副市长张广宁（现任市长）的礼物（中），及赠送给广州市的礼物（左右两片）。

Blue and white sherds salvaged from the Swedish vessel Götheborg, presented by the Swedish Delegation to China as gift to the city of Guangzhou and the then vice mayor, Zhang Guangning in October 2002.

局部

清乾隆青花斗鸡纹盘。1906～1907年瑞典詹姆斯·凯勒先生从"哥德堡号"沉船打捞，2006年7月瑞典国王卡尔十六世·古斯塔夫赠送给广州市人民政府。
Blue and white plate with cockfighting scene, Qianlong Reign, Qing Dynasty. Found by James Keller from the Swedish shipwreck Götheborg from 1906 to 1907. Donated by the Swedish King Carl XVI Gustaf to the Guangzhou Municipality in July 2006.

青花缠枝莲狮纹盖罐，明万历。
Blue and white covered jars with lotus scrolls and a lion. Wanli Reign, Ming Dynasty.

青花"上品香茶"茶叶罐，明崇祯。詹培森先生捐赠。
Blue and white covered tea jars with Chinese characters "上品香茶" (top scented tea). Chongzhen Reign, Ming Dynasty. Donated by Mr. Zhan Peisen.

青花折枝花卉瓜棱形盖罐，明崇祯。
Blue and white melon-form covered jar with floral sprays. Chongzhen Reign,
Ming Dynasty.

青花山水杯，晚明。
Blue and white cups with painted landscape. Late Ming Dynasty.

青玉荷花形执壶，明代。
Tea pot with lotus petals design, Greenish Jade. Ming Dynasty.

五彩龙凤碗，清康熙。
A pair of bowls with wucai motif of dragon and phoenix. Kangxi Reign, Qing Dynasty.

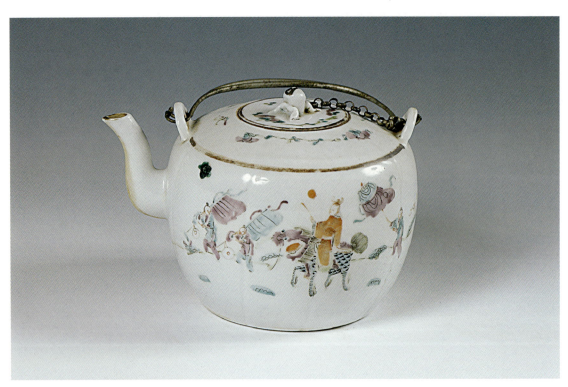

粉彩人物纹提梁壶，清同治。
Handled Tea pot with figures painted in famille rose. Tongzhi Reign, Qing Dynasty.

珊瑚红描金执壶，清同治。
Coral red tea pot with gold decorations. Tongzhi Reign, Qing Dynasty.

青花花鸟纹盖杯，清光绪。
A pair of covered cups and saucers with blue-and-white birds and flowers. Guangxu Reign, Qing Dynasty.

柚木茶圆盒，清代。
Round box made from teak for storing tea, Qing Dynasty.

胭脂红盖杯，20世纪上半叶。
Rouge red covered cups. The first half of the 20th century.

青花花卉纹残片，明嘉靖年间。景德镇青花瓷自元代后期开始外销，至明代已销往亚欧各地。这件马六甲海峡出水的明嘉靖青花花卉纹碟残片，产于景德镇，证明中国瓷器在明代已经从海路销往世界各地。

Shard of dish with flower design in underglaze blue. Jiajing Reign, Ming Dynasty. Jingdezhen blue and white wares began being exported from the late Yuan Dynasty and were sold across both Asia and Europe in the Ming Dynasty. This blue and white shard with floral motif, salvaged in Malacca, was produced in Jingdezhen in the Jiajing Reign of the Ming Dynasty, which proves Chinese porcelain was already sold all over the world in the Ming Dynasty.

清乾隆青花釉里红云龙纹胆瓶，产自景德镇，为外销产品。
Gall-Bladder bottle with underglaze blue and red motif of dragon amongst clouds from Jingdezhen export ware. Qianlong Reign, Qing Dynasty.

清代青花柳亭奶壶，外销品。
Milk jar with blue-and-white landscape. Qing Dynasty. Export Ware.

清代青花花卉"万隆糖果"方罐。罐底有英文Canton、"★广东河南万隆★最好的蜜饯和糖果"字样。
Square jar with Chinese characters "万隆糖果" at bottom and blue-and-white floral motif on body. Qing Dynasty. The English trademark in the ring foot of this jar reads "★MANLOONG HONAM CANTON★BEST PRESERVES AND SWEETMEATS".

青花四季花纹八角形罐，清光绪。底款"万隆糖果"，外销瓷。
Eight-faceted jar marked with Chinese characters "万隆糖果" at bottom and blue-and-white flowers of each season on body. Guangxu Reign, Qing Dynasty. Export Ware.

龙泉窑青釉刻花瓶，明代。
Celadon vase with carved decoration. Longquan ware. Ming Dynasty.

明代龙泉窑青釉菊瓣纹大盘。青釉大盘是元明时期外销瓷的典型产品。
Celadon plate carved with of chrysanthemum petals, Longquan ware, Ming Dynasty. Celadon plate was typical among export wares of the Ming and Qing period.

明代龙泉窑刻梵文大盘。盘心印梵文，外饰两圈弦纹，施梅子青釉。刻印梵文大盘是龙泉窑的外销产品。
Plum-green glazed plate carved with Sanskrit letter at centre, Longquan ware. Ming Dynasty. The letter was encircled by bowstring pattern. Celadon plates with Sanskrit letter were produced for export.

福建德化窑白瓷，釉色洁白莹亮，明清时远销海外。这是明代德化窑
白釉觚（上图）和白釉贴花八角杯（下图）。

Dehua ware was renowned for its luminous, ivory glaze, and was sold overseas in the
Ming and Qing period. These are two Dehua wares: the white-glazed beaker and eight-faceted
white cup with appliqué decoration.

广州府石湾陶瓷不仅行销国内，而且远销海外。这是明末清初石湾窑翠毛釉三足炉。
Shiwan ware from Guangzhou sold well both home and abroad. This three-footed censor coated in kingfisher-feather glaze was made by Shiwan kiln at the turn of Ming to Qing Dynasty.

石湾窑翠毛釉象耳长颈瓶，清代。
Long-necked bottle coated in kingfisher-feather glaze with elephant handles. Shiwan ware. Qing Dynasty.

潮州窑白釉胆瓶，清初。
White glazed gall-bladder bottle. Chaozhou ware. Early Qing Dynasty.

潮州窑白釉狮耳高身瓶，清代。
White-glazed vase with lion handles. Chaozhou ware. Qing Dynasty.

酱釉开光粉彩洋人碗，清乾隆。
Caramel-glazed bowl painted with foreigners in famille rose palette in reserved panels. Qianlong Reign, Qing Dynasty.

清乾隆年间出口欧洲的成套广彩瓷
A set of Canton Enamel exported to Europe, Qianlong Reign, Qing Dynasty.

227

广彩人物包袱瓶，清咸丰。
Jar painted with a wrapping cloth. Canton Enamel ware. Xianfeng Reign, Qing Dynasty.

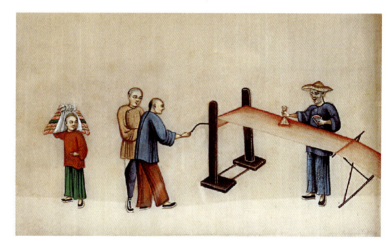

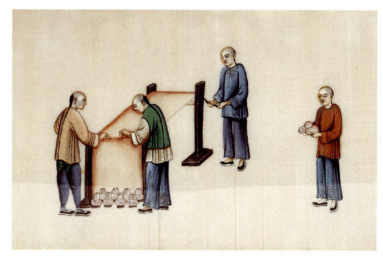

清代通草水彩画上所见的广州丝绸制作程序：养蚕、纺纱、丝织、染色。
The process of producing silk textiles includes raising silkworm, spinning, weaving and dying. Watercolour on pith. Qing Dynasty.

红色花蝶广缎，清代。广缎深受外商喜爱。
　　Red brocade woven with butterflies and petite flowers. Qing Dynasty. Guangzhou brocade woven won great favor among foreign merchants.

（正面）

（背面）

　　威尼斯银币，1964年广州东山韦眷墓出土。韦眷在明成化至弘治年间（1465～1495年）任广州提举市舶师，"纵贾人通诸番，聚珍甚富"。威尼斯银币铸造并通行于15世纪。现今世界上仅存两枚。

　　明清广州中西贸易，除以货易货外，还以外币进行贸易，故乾隆年间广州便有"银钱堆满十三行"之语。在世界经济贸易中，中国靠精美的物产赢得了世界市场，外银不断地流入中国。

Venetian silver coin, excavated from the tomb of a eunuch, Wei Juan, at Dongshan, Guangzhou in 1964. Wei Juan was assigned chief administrator of Canton Custom House during the Chenghua Reign to the Hongzhi Reign (1465~1495), Ming Dynasty. Wei was "a persistent advocator for foreign trade and collected a lot of treasure during his term". This Venetian silver coin, issued and used in the 15th century, is one of two such coins found extant in the world.

Besides the barter trade, Chinese and foreign merchants also traded their goods for foreign currency in Guangzhou during the Ming and Qing period; therefore, Guangzhou witnessed such a thriving business in the Qianlong Reign that it was said that "silver dollars stack up in the 13 Hongs." During the export trade, China sold her exquisite goods to overseas market, and foreign silver currency flooded China with no cease.

孟加拉银币为通行于14～17世纪的印度钱币，1964年广州东山明代韦眷墓出土。

This Bengali silver coin was widely used in India during the 14th to 17th century. It was excavated from Wei Juan's tomb at Dongshan, Guangzhou in 1964.

（正面）

（背面）

西班牙银币，1771年。

Spanish silver coin, issued in 1771.

（正面）

（背面）

（正面）

（背面）

清代，墨西哥银元大量流入中国，在广州等地流通，人称"鹰洋"。这是1894年铸造的墨西哥银元。
Mexican Carolus dollar (aka. eagle dollar) flooded China in the Qing Dynasty, with a circulation in Guangzhou and some other places. These two dollars were cast in 1894.

明清时期，广州货币为铜钱和白银，另有少量的纸币发行。这是1974年西沙礁盘上出土的大明铜钱。

During the Ming and Qing period, currency used in Guangzhou included bronze coins and silver, as well as very few paper notes were issued. These are and bronze coins of the Great Ming excavated from coral reefs in Xisha Islands in 1974.

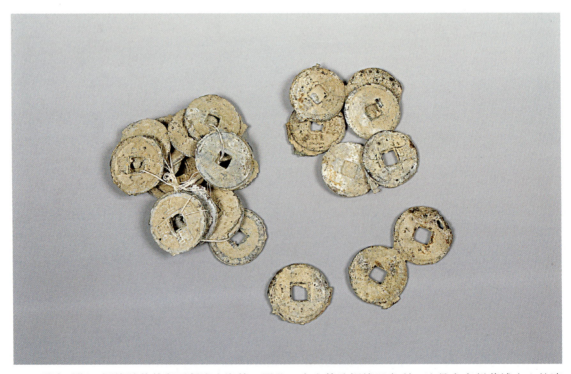

明清时期，铜钱随着外贸不断流出海外，因此，有人伪造铜钱以牟利。这是在广州黄埔出土的清代伪钱。

With bronze coins flooding ceaselessly overseas in the Ming and Qing period, some people cast fake coins to seek profit. These fake coins were excavated from Huangpu, Guangzhou, dated to Qing Dynasty.

　　象牙朝笏，明代南京工部尚书陈绍儒之物。朝笏又名"手板"，是中国古代朝会时手执的狭长板子。《礼记·玉藻》载："笏，天子以球玉，诸侯以象，大夫以鱼须文竹。"象牙为进口物品。明清时期，象牙、犀角、水晶、珊瑚、琥珀、酸枝木、硬木等海外物品源源不断地输入广州，并由广州工匠利用高超技艺，加工制成精致的手工艺品。

　　Ivory court tablet (chao hu in pinyin), once used by Chen Shaoru, the Minister of Works in the Ming Dynasty. Also known as shou ban, a court tablet was a long narrow tablet held by ancient Chinese officials with both hands when going to court. The Chapter Jade Crown, the Record of Rites, says that the King shall use jade court tablet, the princes use ivory and the high-ranked officials, bamboo. During the Ming and Qing period, precious materials were introduced to Guangzhou from overseas, which included ivory, rhinoceros horn, crystal, coral, amber, Siam rosewood and other hard wood. Cantonese artisans made exquisite arts and crafts out of such materials with superb workmanship.

明代犀角杯
Rhinoceros horn cup, Ming Dynasty.

清代水晶光素花瓶（左图）和水晶观音像（右图）
Plain crystal vase and crystal Avalokitesvara, both made in the Qing Dynasty.

清代珊瑚雕桃如意
Coral ruyi-scepter, Qing Dynasty.

清代琥珀扁壶
Amber moonflask, Qing Dynasty.

清代酸枝木嵌螺钿托盘。酸枝木质地细密坚硬，多自东南亚进口，在中国常用来制作上乘家具。
Siam rosewood tray inlaid with mother of pearl. Qing Dynasty. Siam rosewood boasts fine, hard grains and was normally imported from Southeast Asia for making top-class Chinese furniture.

清代紫檀嵌珐琅雕塑人物楼船。广州工匠利用进口硬木制作而成。
Red sandalwood double-decker inlaid with sculpted figures and enamel decorations. Qing Dynasty. The ship was made of imported hardwood by Cantonese craftmen.

得风气之先

First to Accept Western Cultures

明清以来，伴随中西贸易的开展，西方文明传入中国。广州因特殊地位，首先接触和吸收了西方文明。西方科技和西式教育的传入，使广州最早出现了中西合璧式的物品、西式学堂和西式医院。近代工商业的出现，对广州产生了深刻影响，孕育了近代城市时尚，广州人的日常生活、饮食、服饰、婚丧喜庆、宗教信仰等方面有了鲜明的西式色彩。广州成为中国首座得风气之先的城市。

Since the Ming and Qing period, Western Civilizations have been introduced to China along with the growing foreign trade. Because of good location, Guangzhou was the first port that encountered and accepted Western Civilizations. The introductions of Western sciences, technologies and education, made Guangzhou a melting pot of both Occidental and Oriental cultures, with numerous Chinese commodities, schools and hospitals designed as the combination of Chinese and Western. The rise of modern industry and commerce had a great impact on Guangzhou; like a refreshing breeze, it brought fashions to this modern city, with great changes taking place in various fields, such as daily life, meals and drinks, clothes, funerals and weddings, and religions as well ——— all carried a typical Western flavour. Thus, Guangzhou became the first Chinese city that has accepted foreign cultures.

艾约瑟墓碑残件。艾约瑟，1693年来华传教。1707年奉清廷之命，与山西樊守义一同出使罗马教廷。艾约瑟于归途中病逝，被康熙帝"特赐安葬"广州。

Remnant of Joseph-Artoine provana's stone stele. Joseph-Antoine Provana arrived in China as a missionary in 1693. In 1707, he was chosen to accompany Fan Shouyi on a Chinese diplomatic mission to Rome before he died during his return to China. Joseph-Antoine Provana was buried in Canton with the special approval of Emperor Kangxi.

　　圣心大教堂俗名"石室"，位于广州一德路，高57.95米，1863年修建，1888年竣工，由法国工程师稽明章（Guillemin）设计，是我国最大的哥特式石构建筑。
　　Sacred Heart Cathedral. Located on Yide Road of Guangzhou, this Cathedral is constantly referred by the local people as the Seksat, or "House of Masonry". The Cathedral, whick is 57.95m, was built in 1863 and was completed in 1888, it was designed by the French architect Guillemin as the largest Gothic masonwork then in China.

广州圣心大教堂修建时的建筑模型。
Miniature of the Sacred Heart Cathedral, made in Guangzhou in 1863.

石室西式钟盘，原置于石室塔楼顶部。
The face of the Western Clock, originally placed at the top of the House of Masonry tower.

清代铜镀金珐琅花瓶钟。广州钟表业创始于十八世纪初，当地工匠仿照进口的西洋钟表制作自鸣钟，世称"广钟"。广钟在英国机械动力计时器技术的影响下成形，兼具报时和观赏的功能。这个型似中国式花瓶的自鸣钟，绘有当时由欧洲传入的画珐琅彩，表现了中西合璧的制作工艺。

Gilt bronze clock in vase shape and surmounted by flower decorations, Qing Dynasty. The clock-making industry in Guangzhou began in the early 18th century. Clockmakers were able to produce local versions of striking clocks, complete with movements they produced by copying from the English mechanical clockworks. They were known as "Canton clock", and served as both functional timepieces and decorative objects. This striking clock is in the shape of a Chinese vase, and decorated with the painting enamels introduced to China from Europe in the 18th century. It exemplified the mixture of Chinese and Western in craftsmanship.

清代变字开花广钟。报时之际，瓶顶红花盛开，四角绿树转动，钟底出现"喜报长春"。广钟是广州官员的重要贡品。

Cantonese clock with revolving letters and opening flower, Qing Dynasty. When the clock announces the hour, the red flower on top of the vase will open its petals, and the green trees revolves at four corners of the base and Chinese characters "喜报长春" (xi bao chang chun in pinyin, happiness and spring forever) appear at the bottom. Cantonese clock was an important article of tribute to the Qing court from Guangzhou officials.

清代铜镀金卷帘转人广钟。报时之际有音乐伴奏，门帘卷起，红衣女郎绕行一周。
Gilt bronze Cantonese clock with rolling curtain and revolving figure, Qing Dynasty. When announcing the hour, music will be played, with the curtain rolling up automatically and a girl in red circling around the clock.

　　清代鎏金转鸭广钟，每隔15分钟，奏乐一次，亭中人物回旋，一人手捧"招财进宝"祝辞走出，桥上有牧人牵羊，桥下鸭戏清波。
　　Gilt bronze Cantonese clock with revolving duck, Qing Dynasty. Every fifteen minutes, a man in the pavilion will be revolving and another man showing up with a scroll of "招财进宝" (zhao cai jin bao, bring in wealth and treasure), accompanied by music; on the bridge is a shepherd pulling a sheep and below the bridge are ducks swimming in the pond.

　　邹伯奇（1819～1869年），广东南海人，对数学、物理、天文学、地理、器械制造等均有独到的见解和创新之举。1844年，他成功研制了中国第一部照相机，这是他自摄玻璃底片。邹伯奇曾孙邹孟才捐赠。

Zou Boqi (1819～1869), a talent from Nanhai of Canton in modern sciences, was quite familiar with arithmetic, physics, astronomy, geography, and mechanics. He made quite a few mechanic innovations. In 1844, Zou successfully built China's first box camera. This is the glass negative of his self-taken photo. Donated by Zou Mengcai, Zou's great-grandson.

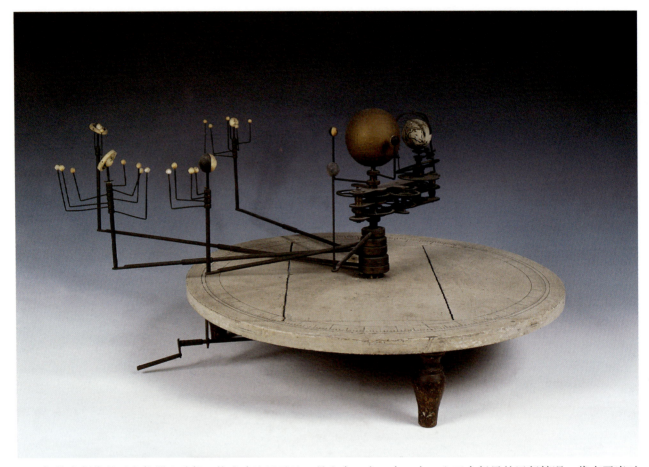

邹伯奇制作的天文仪器七政仪，能准确地显示日、月和水、金、火、木、土五大行星的运行情况，代表了当时中国科技的最高水平。邹伯奇曾孙邹孟才捐赠。

The planet dial made by Zou Boqi can demonstrate accurately the rotation of the fives planets (Venus, Jupiter, Mercury, Mars, and Saturn) around the Sun, as well as the moving trail of the Moon. This dial stands for the highest level of the-then Chinese science and technology. Donated by Zou Mengcai, Zou's great-grandson.

邹伯奇制浑天仪。邹伯奇曾孙邹孟才捐赠。
Armillary sphere made by Zou Boqi. Donated by Zou Mengcai, Zou's great-grandson.

　　冯如（1863～1912年），广东恩平人，中国第一个飞机设计师和飞行家。九岁出洋，苦学飞机制造术。1909年，在美国研制出具有世界先进水平的飞机，后携机回到广州。1912年在广州郊区燕塘进行飞行表演时，不幸失事殉职。

　　Feng Ru (1863～1912), born in Enping County in Guangdong Province on December 15, 1883, is the first aircraft designer and aviator of China. He went overseas at the age of nine and devoted himself to aircraft manufacturing. In 1909, he succeeded in producing a plane then ranked top level in the world before returning to Guangzhou with planes he made by himself. In 1912, Feng Ru died in a plane crash when staging a performance in Yantang, the suburb of Guangzhou City.

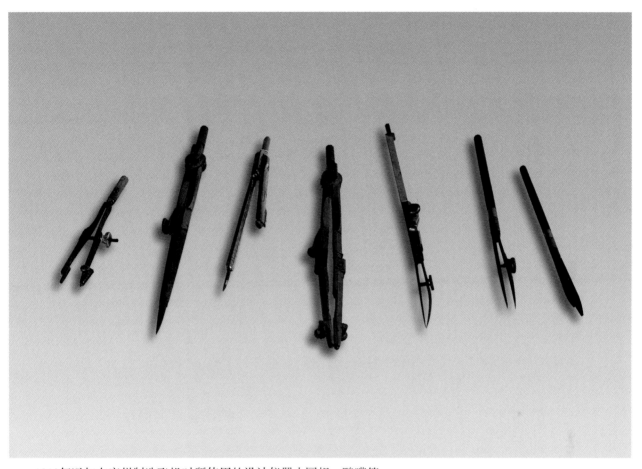

1910年冯如在广州制造飞机时所使用的设计仪器小圆规、鸭嘴笔。
The compasses and the drawing pens designed by Feng Ru when building planes in Guangzhou in 1910.

　　林则徐(1785～1850年)，福建侯官人，在广州禁烟时组织人翻译外文书籍，辑成《四洲志》，被誉为中国"近代放眼看世界第一人"。
　　Lin Tse-Hsu (1785～1850), a native from Houguan of Fujian Province, organized a collection of translations to be compiled to a book *A Gazetteer of Four Continents*. He was deemed the first person of modern China that was "opening eyes to observe the world".

詹天佑（1861～1919年），字眷诚，近代铁路工程专家。幼居广州，12岁留学美国，学习土木工程及铁路专科。1905～1909年设计并主持修建了我国第一条铁路——京张铁路，首创"竖井施工法"和"人"字形线路设计。宣统元年(1909年)商办广东粤汉铁路总公司全体股东选举詹天佑任总办兼总工程师。京张和粤汉这两铁路成就了詹天佑成绩非凡的铁路天涯。

Zhan Tianyou (1861～1919), with a designated name Juancheng, was a renowned railway engineer in modern China. Having spent his childhood in Guangzhou, Zhan studied civil engineering and railway engineering in USA at the age of twelve. From 1905 to 1909, as Chief Engineer of Jingzhang Railway, he invented the double-pronged rail system and was the first who employed the "shaft construction method" to excavate tunnels. In 1909, Zhan was appointed the chief engineer by the shareholders of the private-owned Kwang Tung Yueh-Han Railway Company. The success of both Jingzhang Railway and Yuehan Railway witnessed the remarkable achievement of Zhan's railway constructing career.

　　1864年6月，广州设置了同文馆。这是继1862年7月京师同文馆之后，我国开设最早的同文馆之一。至1900年，广州同文馆先后开设了英文馆、德文馆、日文馆、俄文馆和法文馆，聘请外籍教师担任教官。

　　Tong Wen Guan (School of Combined Learning) was set up at Guangzhou in June of 1864, which was among the earliest imperial translators' colleges established after the Peking Tong Wen Guan. By 1900, various translation courses had been offered to students in Tong Wen Guan, which included English, German, Japanese, Russian and French, all taught by foreign teachers.

广雅书院由清朝两广总督张之洞于1888年创建，校址在西湾路，1889年附设西学堂，1902年改为两广大学堂，开中国传统书院改革先例。1912年改为省立第一中学。

Guang Ya Shu Yuan (literally College of Broadness and Elegance) was founded at Xiwan Road in 1888 by Chang Chih-tung, the viceroy of the two Kwong provinces. In 1889, the Western Study School was added to the College before it was renamed the Great College of Canton and Guangxi in 1902, initiating the reformation of Chinese traditional education. In 1912, the name was changed again for NO. 1 Provincial School.

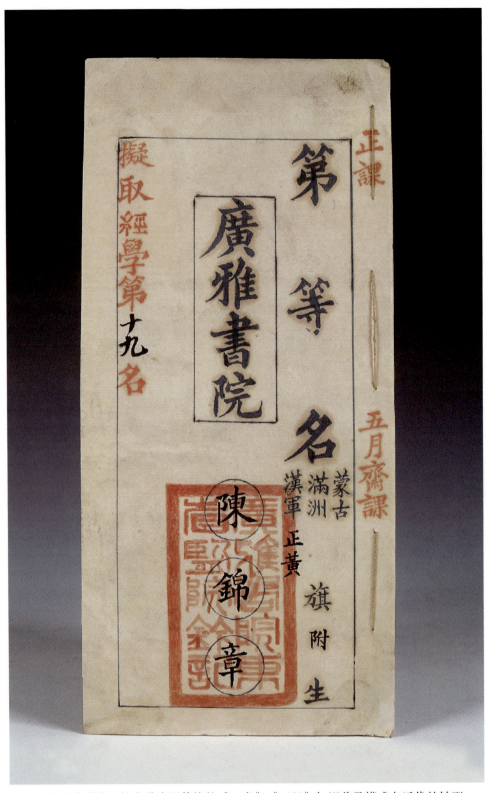

广雅书院课卷，标志着中国传统的《四书》《五经》知识普及模式向近代的转型。
Text book used in Guang Ya Shu Yuan, which marked the education reformation from teaching Chinese traditional studies (i.e. *Four Books of Confucianism* and *Five Classics*) to introducing modern sciences and technologies.

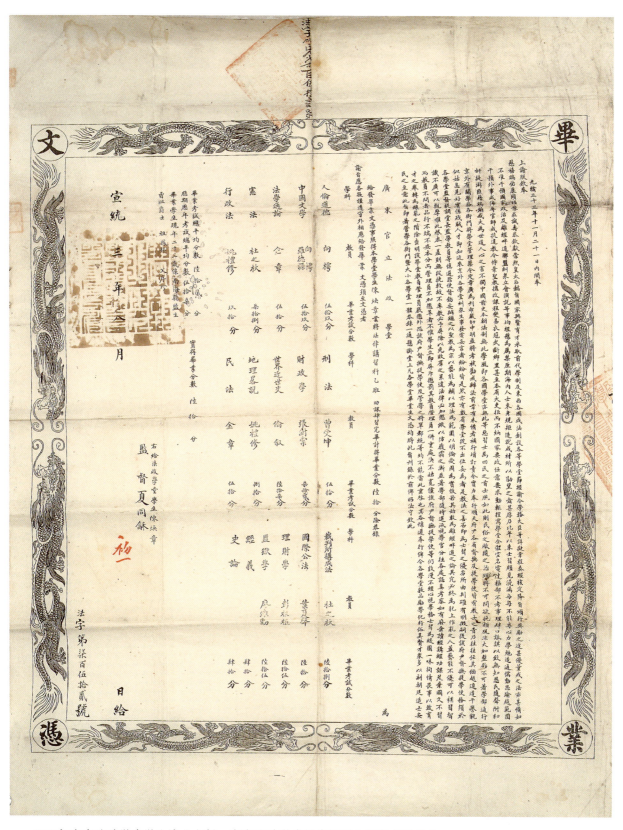

1909年广东法政学堂学生毕业文凭。广东法政学堂是当时国内的新式学堂之一。
Diploma issued in 1909 by Canton Law School, one of the Western schools in China.

陈沃瑞的美国护照及出入美国凭证
US Passport for Chin Yuck Suey

　　1835年11月4日，美国传教士彼得·伯驾在广州十三行内的新豆栏街设立眼科医局，1865年改名为博济医院（今为孙逸仙纪念医院）。它是中国境内第一所西医院。

On November 4th of 1835, American missionary Peter Parker established the Ophthalmic Hospital in Hog Lane, which was later renamed the Canton Hospital (now Sun Yat-Sen Memorial Hospital). It is the first Western medical hospital established in China.

　　方便医院，1899年广州商人在城西兴建方便医所，免费收治重危病人和收殓街头死者，1901年改为城西方便医院，为当时华南最大的慈善机构。
　　Fangbian (convenient) Hospital was founded in 1899 by the local Cantonese merchants in the western part of the city for receiving and treating desperate patients and unclaimed dead bodies free of charge. It was then the largest charitable organization in the South China.

光华医院，1908年由陈子兴、梁培基等一批华人西医生创办。它是中国人自办的第一间西医院。
Guanghua Hospital was established by some Chinese doctors of Western medicine in 1908, including Dr. Chen Zixing and Dr. Liang Peiji. It is the first Western medical hospital founded by Chinese.

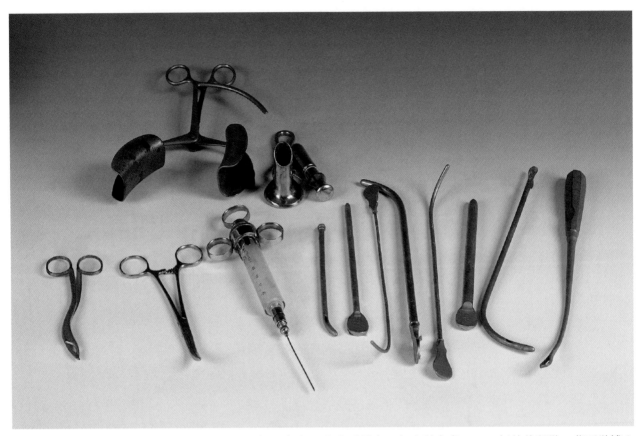

　　梁毅文使用的手术仪器。梁毅文（1903～1991年），广东番禺人，妇产科专家。1929年赴美留学，获医学博士学位。回国后任市柔济医院妇产科主任、夏葛女子医学校代教务长、岭南大学医学院妇产科教授等职。

　　Medical instruments once used by Dr. Liang Yiwen. Liang Yiwen (1903～1991), a native of Fanyu of Canton Province and a renowned gynaecologist, went to study in USA in 1929 before her graduation as a Doctor of Medicine. Upon her return to China, she worked on various posts, including Chief Gynecologist of Hackett Medical Centre, Deputy Dean of the Medical School of Hackett Medical Centre and Professor of Genecology in Canton Christian College.

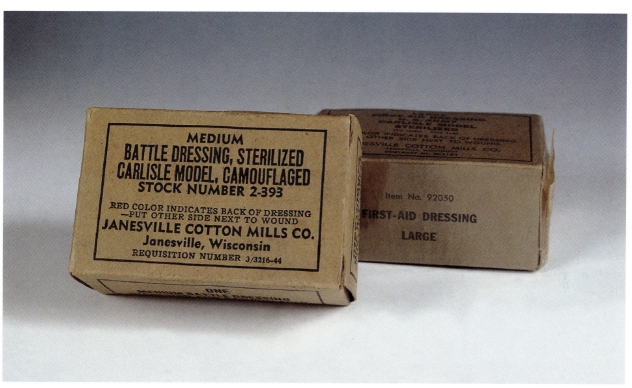

20世纪上半叶方便医院使用的进口绷带（由广州市第一人民医院提供）。
Imported First-Aid Dressing, used in Fangbian Hospital (Convenience Hospital) (Provided by Guangzhou First Municipal People's Hospital).

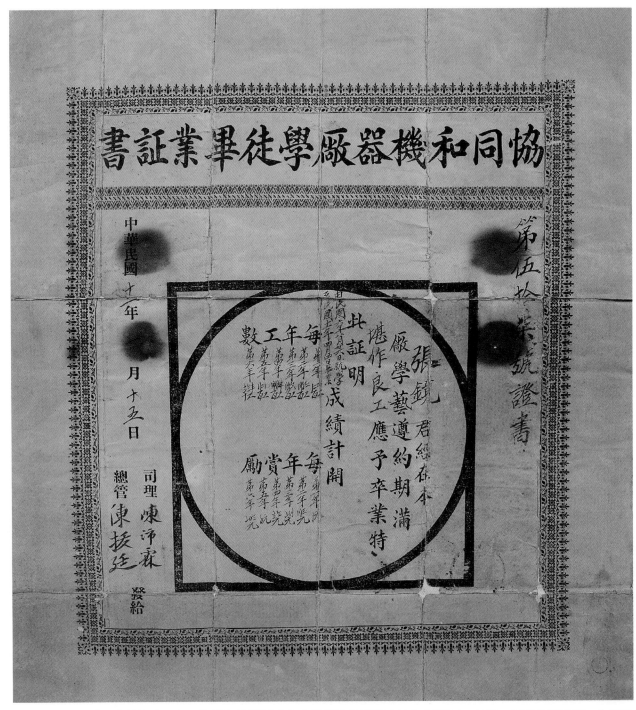

协同和机器厂学徒毕业证书。协同和机器厂（今广州柴油机厂所在地）创建于1912年，制造出我国第一台柴油机。

Certificate of the Completion of the Apprenticeship issued by Xie Tong He Machinery Factory, Xie Tong He Machinery Factory (now Guangzhou Diesel Engine Factory) was established in 1912, in which was produced the first diesel engine in China.

李裕兴针织厂71型锁眼机，20世纪30年代美国胜家厂生产。
Buttonhole sewing machine Type 71, used in Li Yu Xing Knitting Mill, produced by the Singer Sewing Company of U.S.A in 1930s.

李占记钟表行打卡机。李占记钟表行，1912年在文咸东街开办，后在十八甫、惠爱东路开设分行。

Punch-card machine, made by Li Zhan Ji Watchmaker's Shop. The Shop was first opened in Wenxian Dong Street, and later its branches were opened successively on Shi Ba Fu (The 18th Road) and Hui' ai Dong Road.

广州华南风琴厂制造的"双凤牌"手风琴，上有"canton"（广州）字样。
Double Phoenixes Accordion, made by Guangzhou South China Accordion Factory, with the inscription Canton.

20世纪初广东石泉公司玻珠汽水瓶。上有"广东石泉公司"、SAK CHUN & CO.的中英文，以及AERATED WATER、MANUFACTURER、CANTON等字样，瓶内有玻璃珠。

Aerated water bottle containing glass beads, made in the early 20th century. The bottle was inscribed with "SAK CHUN & CO." together with its Chinese name "广东石泉公司", and other English words "AERATED WATER MANUFACTURER CANTON".

"安乐"玻璃汽水瓶，狮纹商标。安乐汽水厂是20世纪初广州发展较快的汽水厂之一。

Bottle of Anle aerated water, with a lion's image as trademark. Anle Aerated Water Factory is one of the fast growing factories that have produced aerated water in the early 20th century.

这是屈臣氏大药房汽水瓶，瓶身有图案及文字。约1828年，英国人A.S.Watson在广州开了家西药房，取名广东大药房。1841年药房迁到香港，并用广东方言将公司名译为"屈臣氏大药房"。20世纪初，广州大药房在广州兼营汽水生意，这也是广州第一个汽水生产企业。

Aerated water bottle, made by A.S. Watsons & Co., with motif and letters. In 1828, A.S. Watson opened a pharmacy in Guangzhou, named Canton Grand Pharmacy. Then it was moved to Hong Kong in 1841, using its Chinese name derived from Cantonese pronunciation of the English name. Besides selling medicine, A.S. Watsons & Co. also produced aerated water, as it is the first company in Guangzhou that did soda water business.

20世纪初先施公司玻璃汽水瓶，上有"粤东先施公司"、"精制卫生汽水"字样。先施公司是1914年澳洲华侨马应彪在广州长堤开设的，是近代广州著名的大百货公司之一。

Aerated water bottle made in the early 20th century, with inscribed Chinese characters "粤东先施公司" (The Sincere Co., East Canton) and "精制卫生汽水" (Refined Clean Aerated Water). Sincere was founded by Mr. Ma Ying Piu, a Chinese Australian, in Changdi of Guangzhou in 1914. It was one of the renowned department stores in Guangzhou in modern times.

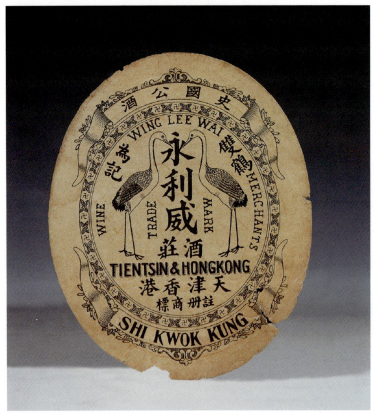

永利威酒厂建于1914年，是广州最早的一家酒厂。这是该厂早期的商标。

Wing Lee Wai Winery was established in 1914 as the first winery in Guangzhou. The picture shows the trademarks used in its early period.

20世纪上半叶销售于广州市场的橄榄形玻璃奶瓶，两边有口，瓶身有MADE IN JAPAN字样，表明是日本制造。
Olive-shaped feeding bottles sold in Guangzhou in the first half of the 20th century, with mouth on both ends and inscribed characters "MADE IN JAPAN".

20世纪初期广州流行的新式女用化妆盒
Ladies' dressing case of the latest type popular in Guangzhou in the early 20th century

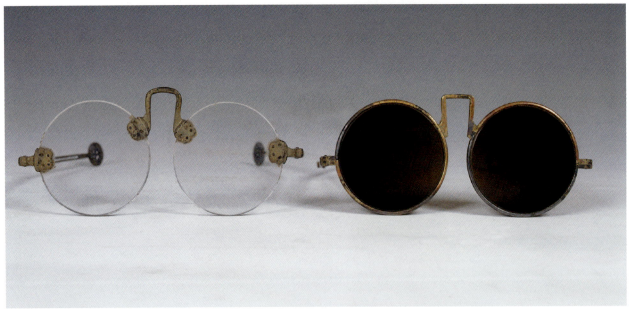

眼镜又称"瑷",明时自海外传入。这是清代嘉庆年间广州生产的水晶眼镜和墨晶眼镜。
Eye glasses were also called ai in pinyin (Chinese character "瑷"), introduced from overseas in the Ming Dynasty. On display are crystal glasses and tawny glasses made in Guangzhou during the Jiaqing Reign of the Qing Dynasty.

木质框玻璃眼镜，1870年制。
Glass optics set in a wooden frame, made in 1870.

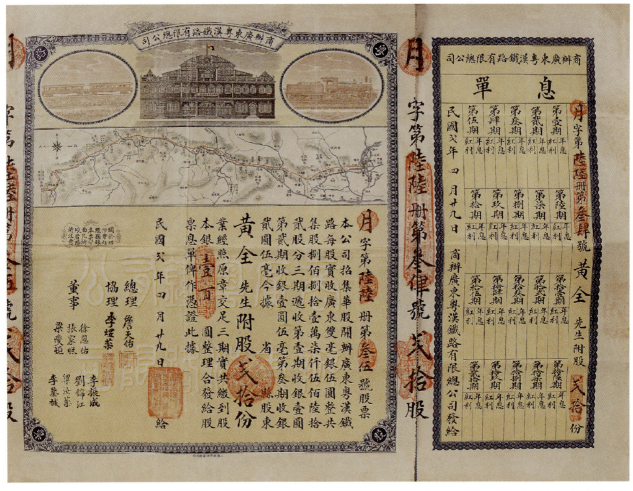

商办广东粤汉铁路有限公司的股票、息单。广东商办粤汉铁路公司成立于1906年。1911年清政府宣布铁路国有后，粤汉铁路公司是全国唯一属商办的铁路股份，1925年广东革命政府将其改为官督商办。

The stock and the dividend warrant issued by Canton Yuet Han Railway Co. Ltd. Yuet Han Railway Co. Ltd. was established by Cantonese merchants in 1906. In 1911 the Qing government declared that all railways in China, except for Yuet Han Railway who has private stocks, must belong to the State. In 1925, the Canton Revolutionary Government changed the way of running this Company to government supervised and merchants managed.

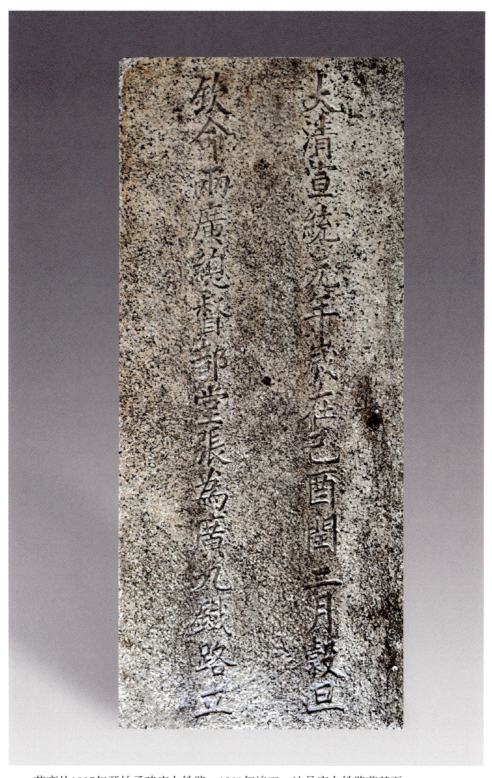

英商从1907年开始承建广九铁路，1911年竣工。这是广九铁路奠基石。

The construction of Guangzhou-Kowloon Railway started in 1907 on the money invested by British merchants and it was completed in 1911. This is the foundation stone laid for the Railway.

1919年广州珠江电船有限公司发行的股票
Stock issued by the Guangzhou Pearl River Electric Boat Co. Ltd. in 1919.

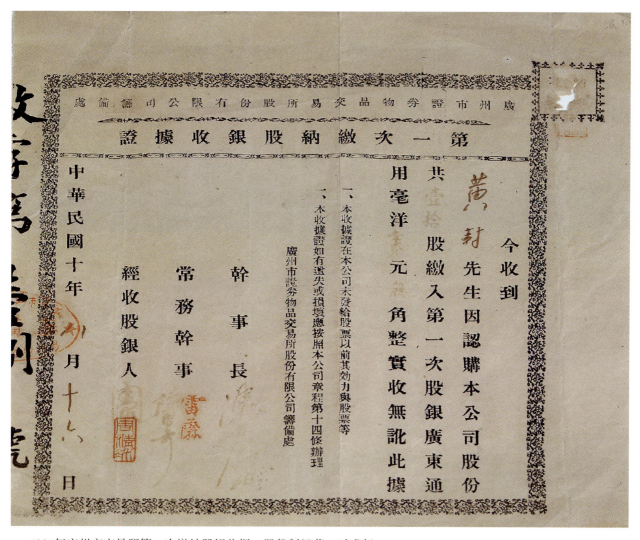

1921年广州市交易所第一次缴纳股银收据，股份制经营一时盛行。
The receipt of the payment for the stocks, offered by Guangzhou Municipal Stock Exchange in 1921 when joint-stock companies gained a wide popularity.

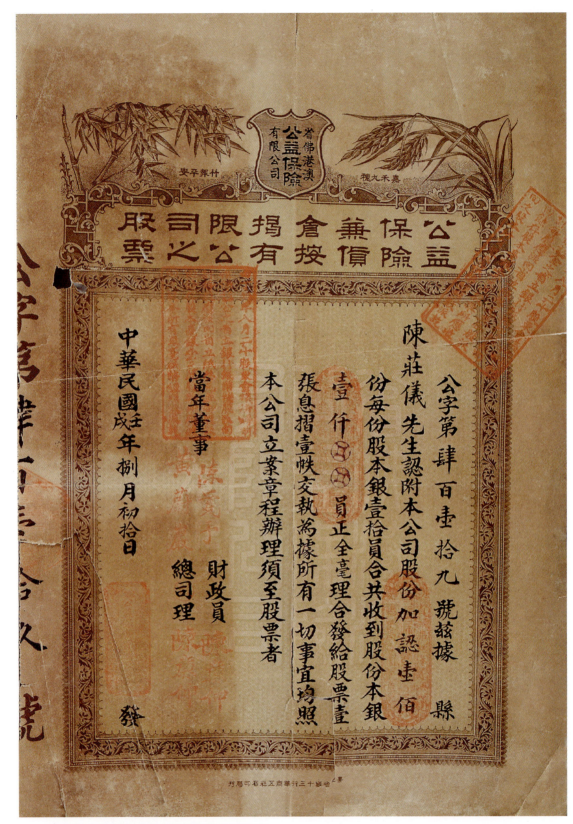

1922年公益保险兼货仓按揭有限公司股票
Stock of the Public Welfare Insurance and Storage Mortgage Co. Ltd, issued in 1922.

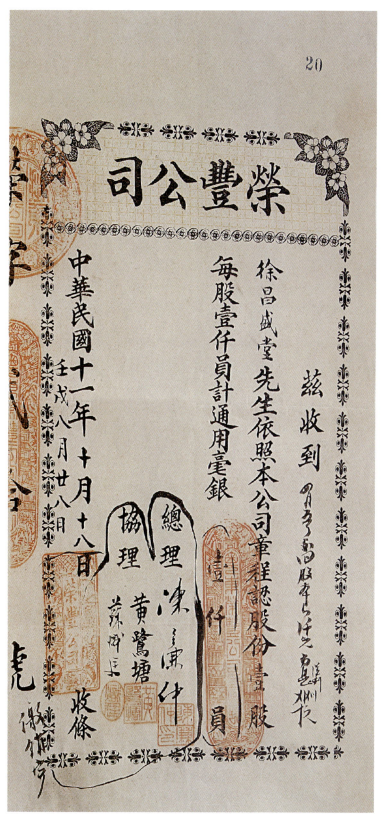

1922年荣丰公司股票
Stock of Rong Feng Co. Ltd. issued in 1922

1932年沙面电报局电报，上盖沙面电报局章。
Telegraph from the Shamian Telegraph Office in 1932, with the Office's Seal Mark.

1933年中国银行汇票（英文版）
Draft of Bank of China (English version) used in 1933

1934年中国银行汇票（英文版），背面加盖沙面太古洋行印等。
Draft of Bank of China (English version) used in 1934, with a seal mark of Swire Bank on the reverse.

1934年中国银行汇票（英文版），背印香港汇丰银行和香港中国银行广州办事处经营人员印章及盖章印，封面有TRANSFER转帐印。
Draft of Bank of China (English version) used in 1934. On the reverse it shows a HSBC seal mark, a seal mark of the Guangzhou Office of Bank of China Hong Kong, and a private seal of the Office's clerk. On the converse is put the seal of TRANSFER.

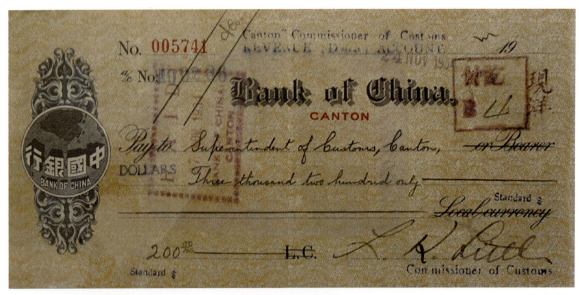

1934年中国银行汇票（英文版），加盖粤海关监督关防印。
Draft of Bank of China (English version) used in 1934, with the seal that says "Supervised by Canton Custom House".

广州自动电话总局，1903年广州始设电话总局于雨帽街，1928年在丰宁路设自动电话总局。
Guangzhou Telephone Bureau was set up in 1903 on Yumao Street, and later a Self-dial Telephone Bureau was established in 1928 on Fengning Road.

　　20世纪初流行于广州的手摇电话机，黑色塑胶话柄，木座，没有号码盘dial装置，所有的通话均通过接线员进行。1903年广州设电话总局，总机系磁石牌式。1928年改设自动电话。
Handset telephone popular in Guangzhou in the early 20th century, with black bakelite handle and a wooden stand. The telephone had no dial as all communication went through the operator. In 1903, the General Telephone Office was established in Guangzhou, with a magneto exchange, followed by the rising of the automatic dial telephone in 1928.

　　19世纪90年代，留声机在欧美等国家投入使用。这是19世纪末流行于广州的旧式留声机，由美国哥伦比亚生产，木座，铜喇叭，深受当时上层社会的青睐。

Gramophone was put into use in Europe and America in 1890s. This old-style gramophone, produced by Columbia, USA, was extremely favoured by the upper class of Guangzhou by the end of the 19th century. It has a wooden base and a copper horn.

　　20世纪初，西方国家发明了收音机。这台收音机是由英国制造的，上有
BUSH RADIO、LONDON ENGLAND、A.C.MAINS RECEIVERS、TYPE
EBS3等标志，在20世纪初年收音机已出现在广州人的生活中。

　　In the early 20th century, radio was invented in the West. This radio was made in England, on which were inscribed English words "BUSH RADIO, LONDON ENGLAND, A. C. MAINS RECEIVERS, TYPE EBS3". It proves that early in the 20th century radio already went into Guangzhou people's life.

　　该灯罩为钕玻璃制造，上有SIEMENS标志。这是20世纪初已经流行于广州家庭中的由世界上最大的德国西门子公司生产的灯罩。

　　The lampshade is made of neophane glass, branded SIEMENS. This shows that lampshades, often seen in Guangzhou households in the early 20th century, were then produced by the largest company of the world, Siemens.

清宣统三年（1911年）广州生产的水压消防车。车体为木，刻有"真庆宫 宣统三年"及"永隆制造"等字样。车中间有水泵，靠横杆加压出水。这种原理应出自英国。

Pumper made in Guangzhou in the third year of the Xuantong Reign, Qing Dynasty. In the wooden carriage were inscribed "Zhenqing Gong, the third Year of Xuantong Reign" and "Made by Yonglong". A pump is installed in the middle of the carriage for pressing water through a lever. The operation principle of this pumper shall have come from the England.

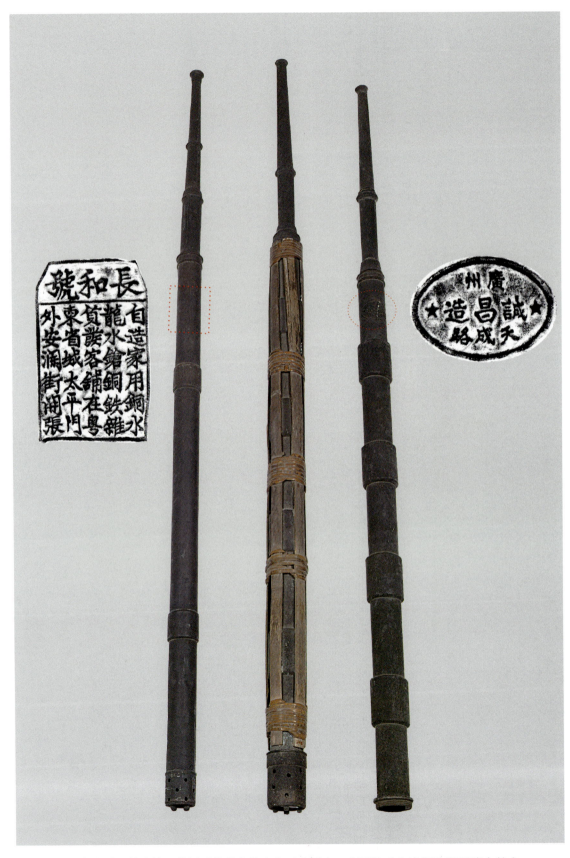

广州生产的手压救火枪。使用时将救火枪直立于水桶中，上下拉动上半部分即可喷水救火。
Pump-action Shotgun made in Guangzhou. A back and forward motion of a sliding lever operated by hand, will eject water out of a water barrel, where the shotgun is laid erect.

1934年广州铸铁沙井盖
Cast iron well cover used in Guangzhou in 1934

　　这是20世纪初广州民间所用产自新加坡的铜熨斗，上书"德记号自造"。当时珠江三角洲地区与东南亚的联系比较密切。
Copper iron used in Guangzhou households in the early 20th century, made in Singapore with a Chinese inscription "Made by De Ji Firm". This iron reflects the close contact between Pearl River Delta and Southeast Asia.

铜熨斗，20世纪初流行于广州家庭。
Copper iron, popular in Guangzhou households in the early 20th century.

　　煤油炉又称火油灯，清末已经在广州出现，20世纪初在广州流行。其灯身有英文"PHOEBUS"（太阳神意）和"TRADEMARK"。

　　Kerosene stove, also named kerosene lamp, first appeared in China at the end of the Qing dynasty and was popular in Guangzhou in the early 20th century. The English words "PHOEBUS" and "TRADEMARK" can be found on the base.

西洋音乐深受广州上层社会喜爱，这是20世纪早期广州使用的西洋喇叭形小号。
Western music was favoured by the upper class of Guangzhou. This is a trumpet seen in Guangzhou in the early 20th century.

九子全盒
Snack box with nine partitions inside

20世纪30年代广州学生用藤笈
School rattan case in 1930s

玉兰花壁灯
Wall lamp in the shape of magnalia flower

这是20世纪早期广州人使用的木制雪柜，是现代冰箱的雏形。
Wooden fridge used by Cantonese in the early 20th century. It is deemed the proto-type of the contemporary fridge.

1935年广州第一次集体婚礼合影，新人们身着西式结婚礼服，反映了西方文化对广州的影响。

A group photo taken at the first group wedding organized in Guangzhou in 1935 when brides and bridegrooms were dressed in Western style. The photo reflects the impact of Western culture on Guangzhou.

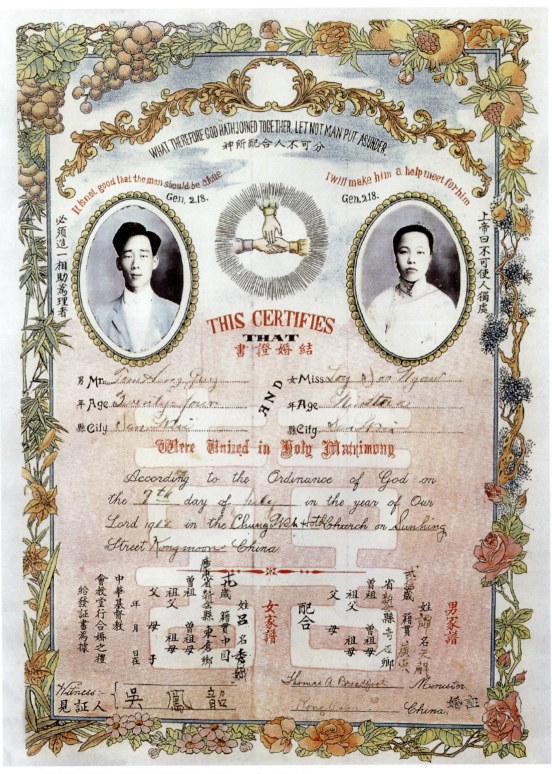

20世纪初的华人基督徒结婚证书（谭士文博士提供）。
Marriage Lines of a Chinese Christian couple in the early 20th century(Provided by Dr. Romon Tom).

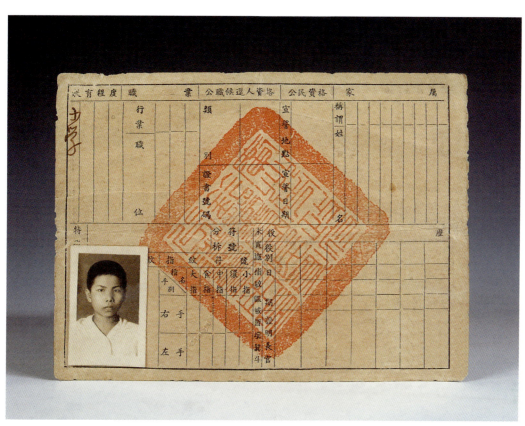

1949年广州市民身份证
ID of a Guangzhou Citizen in 1949

1936年广州市政府土地不动产登记证
Real Estate Certificate issued by Guangzhou Municipality in 1936

　　清末民初，原兴起于地中海沿岸地区的"骑楼"传进广州。因它适应岭南气候，又便于做生意，很快流行于粤北、粤东、粤西和广西等地商埠。它具有古希腊罗马柱范、阿拉伯式穹顶、哥特式塔尖等特征，又与岭南传统建筑相结合，中西合璧，充分显示出广州对多元文化的兼融性。

　　Tsi-Lo (Sotto Portico) was introduced to Guangzhou at the turn of the Qing dynasty and the Republic of China. As an architectural style originally from the Mediterranean, Tsi-Lo won a wide popularity in the North, the East, and the West of Canton and also Guangxi because it goes with the Lingnan climate and facilitate doing business. Mixture of Greek and Roman pillars, Arabian dome and Gothic pinnacle, it also accommodated Lingnan architectural elements. Tsi-Lo reflects the diverse cultures in Guangzhou's character.

英 雄 城 市
Heroic Metroplis

　　广州是一座富有革命优良传统的英雄城市。中国近代史始于广州，中国人民反抗西方侵略斗争也始于广州。近代广州，得领风气之先，积极进取，开物成务，是维新思想的启蒙地，中国民主革命的策源地和国民革命中心。1927年12月爆发的广州起义是中国共产党在城市建立苏维埃政权的大胆尝试。抗日战争时期，广州人民在中国共产党的领导下，以各种形式抗击日本侵略者，最终取得抗战的胜利。国民党政府发动内战后，广州爱国民众在中国共产党领导下，开展和推动爱国民主运动，恢复和壮大人民武装斗争，1949年10月14日，迎来广州解放。

　　Guangzhou, a heroic city with traditional spirits of revolution，is where the modern history of China and Chinese people's resistance to the West aggression started. As the Southern window of China, Guangzhou is featured by its enthusiastic and enterprising spirits as well as the innovative ethos, which makes Guangzhou the cradle of the bourgeois reforming thoughts, the base of democratic revolutionary campaigns and the center of national revolution. The Guangzhou Uprising in December 1927 was a fearlessly move of the CCP's (Chinese Communist Party) trying to establish a city-base soviet regime. During the period of the Anti-Japanese War, Guangzhou citizens, led by CCP, fought against the invasive Japanese in various forms, which was finally ended by a victory. Again under the leadership of CCP, Guangzhou patriots carried out patriotic and democratic movements, resumed and strengthened people's armed struggles after the Kuomintang launched the Civil War. On October 14, 1949, Guangzhou was liberated.

三元里村民抗英武器。鸦片战争时期，广州人民积极支持林则徐禁烟，三元里村民还联合附近乡民，集聚在三元古庙前，举起三星旗，誓师抗英。

Weapons used by the Sanyuanli villagers in their anti-British fight. During the Opium War, Guangzhou people gave great support to Lin Zexu's ban on opium addicting and trading. At the same time, the Sanyuanli villagers united the neighboring villagers and gathered in front of the Sanyuanli Temple, holding high the Three-star Banner and taking an oath to resist the British invaders.

梁启超致康有为函。广州是康有为、梁启超维新思想的启蒙地。
Letter from Liang Qichao to Kang Youwei. Guangzhou is the cradle of Liang and Kang's reforming thoughts.

中国民主革命先行者孙中山全身像
Sun Yat-sen, forerunner of Chinese democratic revolution.

石狮子。1911年4月 27日（农历三月廿九日）， "三·二九" 起义爆发。革命党人在进攻两广总督署时，与清兵展开了枪战。总督署门前的两个石狮子上，留下了23处弹痕，其中一处在狮子的眼睛上，至今清晰可辨。

Stone lions in front of the Residence of the Governor-general. On April 27, 1911, the Huanghuagang Uprising broke out. On their way to attack the Residence of the Governor-general, revolutionaries had gun fights against Qing forces, which left 23 bullet scratches on the stone lions. One of the scratches, until now, can be still easily seen on one of the lion's eyes.

纪念辛亥革命胜利茶壶
Teapot commemorating the success of the 1911 Revolution

　　孙中山手书"志在冲天"横幅。广州是孙中山护法运动的大本营，孙中山及其革命战友先后三次在广州建立革命政权，开展革命活动。孙中山一生倡导航空救国，这是他表彰杨仙逸而手书的横幅。

Horizontal scroll by Sun Yat-sen. Guangzhou was the headquarters of the Doctrine Defending Movement. Sun Yat-sen, together with his revolutionary partners, established revolutionary regime in Guangzhou three times in succession. In all his life, Sun advocates the important role of aviation industry in saving a country. This is the scroll he honored Yang Xianyi (the father of the China Air Force) with.

41

第三次全國大會宣言

中國人民受外國及軍閥兩層暴力的壓迫，國家生命和人民自由都危險到了極點，不但工人農民學生感覺者，即和平穩健的商人也漸漸感覺着了。

目前北京政局之紛亂兒戲；北洋軍閥統治之下工會學生會日在壓迫摧殘中；山東河南兵匪之猖獗；外人之藉端要挾，并要拿回華盛頓會議所賞的利益；沙市長沙日本水兵之暴行；外人強合棉花出口；吳佩孚齊燮元爭相製造廣東之戰禍；吳佩孚蕭耀南合力助成川亂；又若未來的奉直戰爭及直系軍閥之內閧；——在在可以證明內憂外患更復加於國民之身，除集合國民自己之勢力，做強大的國民自決運動，別無他途可以自救；也在在可以證明本黨一年以來號召的：「打倒軍閥」「打倒國際帝國主義」之國民革命運動，不是一條錯誤的道路。

中國國民黨應該是國民革命之中心勢力，更應該立在國民革命之領袖地位。 不幸中國國民黨常有兩個錯誤的觀念：（一）希望外國援助中國國民革命，這種求救於敵的辦法，不但失了國民革命領袖的面目，而且引導國民依趨外力，滅殺國民獨立自信之精神；（二）集

中共三大宣言。1923年6月，中国共产党第三次全国代表大会在广州召开，中共广东区委负责大会的筹备工作并派代表出席大会。

Declaration of the Third National Congress. In June 1923, the Third National Congress of CCP was held in Guangzhou. The Guangdong District Committee of the CCP took charge of the preparations and presented their representatives in the meeting.

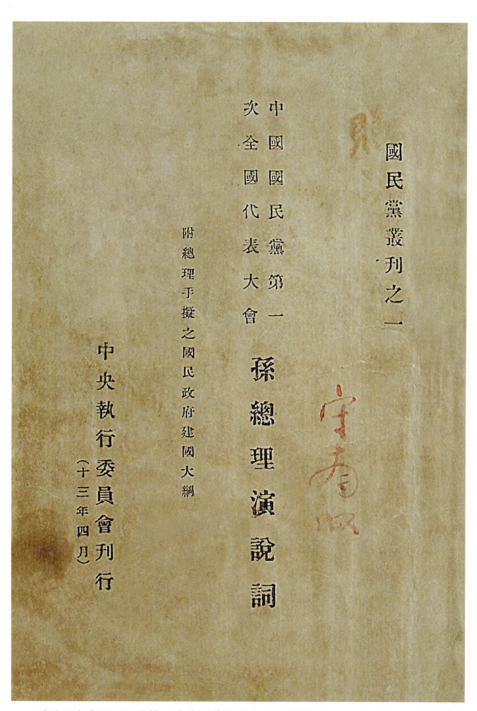

國民黨叢刊之一

中國國民黨第一次全國代表大會

孫總理演說詞

附總理手擬之國民政府建國大綱

中央執行委員會刊行
（十三年四月）

孙总理在中国国民党第一次全国代表大会上的演说词。1924年1月，中国国民党
第一次全国代表大会在广州召开。
Premier Sun' s speech at Kuomintang' s First Party Congress held in Guangzhou in January 1924.

黄埔军校干部教导队毕业纪念章。为建立革命军队，孙中山于1924年在广州创办了黄埔军校。
Drillmaster's Cockade of the Whampoa Military Academy. In order to organize his own revolutionary force, Sun Yat-sen set up the Whampoa Military Academy in Guangzhou in 1924.

广州起义者杨馨坤佩戴过的红布带。1927年12月，中共广东省委领导的广州起义爆发，这次起义是中国共产党在城市建立苏维埃政权的大胆尝试。
Red scarf used by Yang Xinkun during the Guangzhou Uprising. In December 1927, the Guangdong Provincial Committee of the CCP launched the Guangzhou Uprising. This is a fearlessly move of the CCP's trying to establish a city-base soviet regime.

315

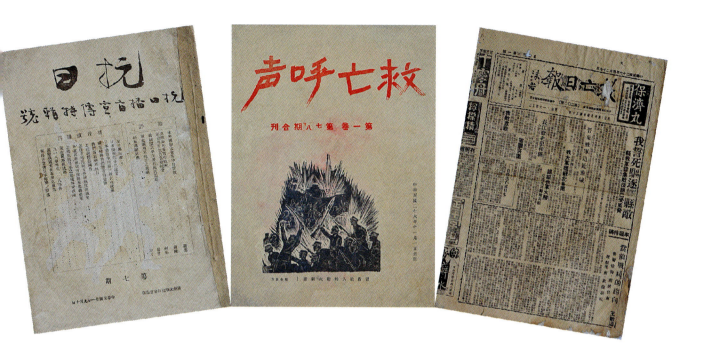

　　抗日救亡刊物。"九一八"事变后，广州各界爱国民众在中共领导下积极开展抗日示威游行，组织抗日游击队，建立农村抗日游击根据地，开展武装斗争，最终取得抗日战争的胜利。

　　Publications issued during the Anti-Japanese War. After the September Eighteenth Incident, patriots from different circles, led by CCP, held demonstrations to condemn the Japanese invaders, organized anti-Japanese guerrilla forces, set up Anti-Japanese bases in rural areas and carried out struggles against the Japanese invaders, all of which were concluded in a final victory.

珠江纵队中山特派室委任令
Letter of Attorney from Zhongshan Special Commission of Zhujiang Detachment

1945年9月16日，日军受降代表田中久一在广州中山纪念堂签署投降书。
On September 16, 1945, Japanese Commander Tanaka Hisakazu signed the treaty of surrender in the Sun Yat-sen Memorial Hall in Guangzhou.

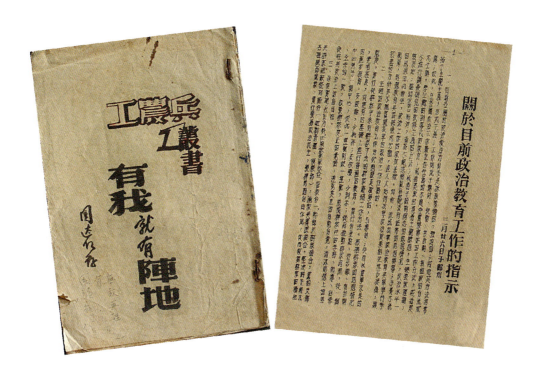

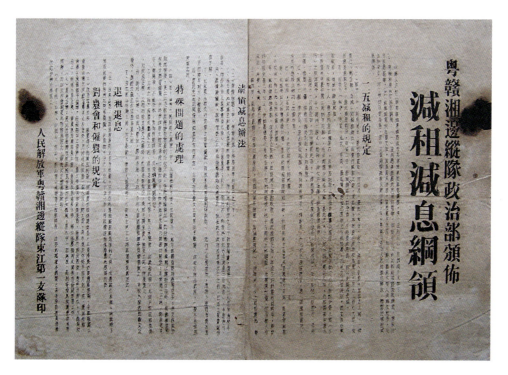

　　宣传刊物《关于目前政治教育工作的指示》、《减租减息纲领》、《有我就有阵地》。抗战胜利后，国民党政府发动内战，在中国共产党领导下，广州各界民众开展爱国民主运动，广州郊区的人民武装斗争得到恢复和壮大。

　　Propagandistic publications issued during the Civil War period. After the Anti-Japanese War, the Kuomintang launched the Civil War. Guangzhou patriots from different circles, led by CCP, carried out democratic and patriotic movements. Armed struggles were resumed and enlarged around Guangzhou at the same time.

1949年10月1日中国共产党中央华南分局印发的《告广东人民书》
Speech to Guangdong People

新中国成立后广州升起的第一面五星红旗

The first Five-Starred Red Flag erected in Guangzhou after the establishment of the People's Republic of China.

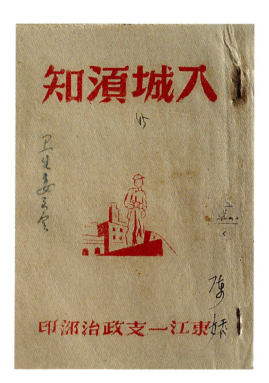

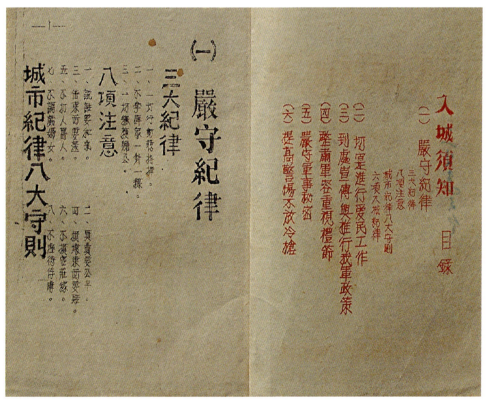

人民解放军《入城须知》
Notice of Entering Guangzhou City of PLA(Chinese People's Liberation Army)

1949年10月14日，广州解放。图为人民解放军攻占国民政府行政院。
On October 14, 1949, Guangzhou was liberated. The PLA (Chinese People's Liberation Army) troops occupied the temporary seat of the States Council of Guomindang Government.

广州历史大事记

约五、六千年前，广州的先民——古越人，已在广州繁衍生息，生产工具以石器、陶器、骨器为主，从事渔猎和农业生产。

公元前214年　秦始皇平定岭南，将岭南地区纳入秦帝国版图，设置南海、桂林、象三郡。南海郡治番禺，即今广州。广州建城自此始。

公元前204年　赵佗建立南越国，定都番禺，自称南越武王。

公元前111年　汉武帝平定南越国，分南越国土为南海等九郡，南海郡治番禺。

公元226年　三国东吴孙权设交、广二州，合浦以南为交州，合浦以北为广州，"广州"由此得名。

公元917年　刘岩在广州建立大越国，国号汉，史称南汉。

公元1068～1077年　广州大规模修建城垣，修建了东、西、子三城。

公元1380年　广州扩建城垣，合宋代三城为一体，把广州城北部扩展到越秀山，并建造镇海楼。

公元1646年　朱聿粤在广州自立为帝，年号绍武，史称南明。

公元1839年6月　钦差大臣林则徐在虎门销毁鸦片。

公元1840年6月　英国发动对华战争，第一次鸦片战争爆发。

公元1841年5月30日　广州城北发动了三元里人民抗英斗争。这是近代中国民间第一次有组织的武装抗击外国侵略者的斗争。

公元1856年10月　英法联军再次侵占广州，第二次鸦片战争爆发。

公元1911年4月27日（农历三月二十九日）　同盟会在广州发动了辛亥"三·二九"起义，又称"黄花岗起义"，揭开了辛亥革命的序幕。

公元1911年11月17日　广州都督府在广州成立，史称"广州光复"。

公元1917年　中华民国军政府在广州成立，孙中山就任大元帅。

公元1918年10月19日　广州市政公所宣布拆城墙、开马路。

公元1921年2月15日　广州市政厅成立，孙科任广州第一任市长，是为广州建市之始。

公元1923年6月10日～20日　中国共产党在广州召开第三次全国代表大会。

公元1924年1月20～30日　中国国民党在广州召开第一次全国代表大会。

公元1926年　毛泽东主持第六届农民运动讲习所。

公元1927年12月11日　中国共产党在广州发动了"广州起义"。

公元1945年9月16日　侵粤日军签字投降仪式在广州中山纪念堂举行，标志着广东人民抗日斗争的全面胜利。

公元1949年10月14日　广州解放。10月28日，广州市人民政府成立，叶剑英任市长。

公元1978年　广东实行改革开放政策。

公元1992年　邓小平南巡，抵达深圳，加大改革力度。

Historical Highlights of Guangzhou

As early as five to six thousand years ago, the ancestors of Guangzhou-Yue people have settled here and conducted fishing, hunting and agricultural activities with tools made of tone, pottery and bone.

214B.C.　The First Emperor of Qin conquered Lingnan area, which has been at the first time annexed into the Qin Empire. Three prefectures, Nanhai, Guilin and Xiang were set up and Nanhai Prefecture established its capital in Panyu, nowadays Guangzhou.

204B.C.　Zhao Tuo set up Nanyue Kingdom and crowned himself the Emperor Wu of Nanyue with Panyu as its capital.

111B.C.　Emperor Wu of the Han Dynasty annihilated the Nanyue Kingdom and divided its territory into nine prefectures, among which is the Nanhai Prefecture with Panyu as its capital.

A.D.226　Sun Quan of the Wu Kingdom during the Three Kingdoms period designated the area to the south of Hepu as Jiaozhou and the area to its north as Guangzhou. The term "Guangzhou" appeared at the first time.

A.D.917　Liu Yan set up the Kingdom of Great Yue, named Han Dynasty, which was later referred to by scholars as Southern Han Dynasty.

A.D.1068～1077　The city of Guangzhou underwent significant reconstructions and three small cities-the east, west and the central cities were built during that period.

A.D.1380　The three small cities built in Guangzhou were amalgamated and expanded northward to Yuexiu Mountain, on the top of which Sea-dominating Tower was built.

A.D.1646　Zhu Yuyue inaugurated the Shaowu Dynasty in Guangzhou, known in the history "the Southern Ming Dynasty".

A.D.1839　The imperial commissioner Lin Zexu destroyed opium in Humen.

A.D.1840　The British government took military action against China, and the First Opium War broke out.

A.D.1841　The Sanyuanli villagers fought against the British invaders, marking the first success of organized civil struggle against the foreign invasion in the modern history of China.

A.D.1856　Allied forces of English and French attacked and occupied Guangzhou again, and the Second Opium War was on.

A.D.1911　The Chinese Revolutionary League launched the Huanghuagang Uprising, heralding beginning of the Xinhai Revolution in the year of 1911.

A.D.1911　The Military Government of Guangzhou was set up, known in the history "Recovery of Guangzhou".

A.D.1917　Guangzhou Parliament set up with Sun Yat-sen as elected President.

A.D.1918　The City Council of Guangzhou began to dismantle old city walls and built roads.

A.D.1921　The City Hall of Guangzhou set up and Sun Ke was designated as the first Mayor of Guangzhou. The modern Guangzhou City was, at the first time, established formally.

A.D.1923　The Third National Congress of the Communist Party of China was held in Guangzhou.

A.D.1924   The First National Congress of the Guomindang Group (National Party) was held in Guangzhou.

A.D.1926   Mao Zedong is elected as the Director of the Canton Peasant Movement Institute.

A.D.1927   The Chinese Communist Party launched the "Guangzhou Uprising".

A.D.1945   Japanese forces in Guangzhou surrendered in the Sun Yat-sen Memorial Hall, marking the final victory of the anti-Japanese struggles of Guangzhou people.

A.D.1949   The People's Liberation Army entered Guangzhou. The municipal government was established with Ye Jianying as the Mayor.

A.D.1978   The policy of reform and opening to the outside world was launched in Guangdong.

A.D.1992   Deng Xiaoping visited Guangdong and Shenzhen to push his Reform Policy.

广州对外海上交通大事记

公元前110～前87年　汉武帝遣使从南方大港入南海，远达今印度洋斯里兰卡。

公元2年　黄支国（今印度）经海路向中国进献犀牛。

公元166年　大秦国（古罗马帝国）使臣经海路到广东登岸，送来象牙及犀角等贡物，是为罗马帝国与中国经海路的首次交往。

公元231年　三国吴帝孙权遣朱应和康泰出使南洋诸国。

公元281年　罗马帝国遣使访问中国，经广州至洛阳。

公元397年～401年　僧人昙摩耶舍从罽宾国（今印度）到广州传教，在光孝寺内创建大雄宝殿。

公元412年　法显西行求佛法后，随商船经广州返抵青州（今山东省）。

公元527年　印度僧人达摩循海路至广州，登岸后建"西来庵"，后人称他上岸的地方为"西来初地"。

公元7世纪　广州市成为一个重要的外贸中心。伊斯兰教经海路传入中国，并率先在广州传播。

公元661年　唐朝政府在广州设置市舶使，总管东南海路邦交贸易，其机构称"市舶使院"。

公元671年　僧人义净在广州乘波斯船舶泛海西行求佛法。

公元8世纪　阿拉伯人在广州筑建了中国现存最早的清真寺——怀圣寺。

公元747年～749年　唐朝政府在广州城西划地设"蕃坊"，专供阿拉伯及波斯的侨民居住。

公元785年～804年　宰相贾耽记载了"广州通海夷道"，证明以广州为始发港的海上丝绸之路，此时已延伸至波斯湾一带。

公元971年　宋灭南汉，于广州设置市舶司，作为总管海贸机构。

公元982年　摩逸国（今菲律宾）商船前来广州贸易，是为历史记载菲律宾与广州贸易的开通。

公元1071年　层拔国（今桑给巴尔岛）贡使循海路至广州，证明宋代的对外交通已远达东非。

公元1080年　宋朝政府制订《元丰广州市舶条》，是为中国最早的市舶管理条例。

公元1286年　元朝政府在广州首置市舶都转运司。

公元1405年　明廷设置浙江、福建和广东三市舶司，管理朝贡贸易。在广州十八甫建怀远驿，用以招待外国贡使和蕃商。

公元1509年　暹罗（今泰国）蕃舶因飓风漂流至广东，当地官员对货品征税后允许贸易，从此广东正式建立了蕃舶的课税制度。

公元1522年　明廷因倭寇为患，罢浙江及福建两市舶司，广东和广州成为当时唯一的通商地区和口岸。

公元1555年～1566年　葡人以澳门为中转港，开辟了广州—澳门—果亚里斯本的远洋航线，全程11，890海里。

公元1583年　意大利传教士利玛窦由澳门入广东肇庆传教。

公元1685年　清廷宣布广州、松江、宁波和厦门为对外贸易港口，设立粤、江、浙、闽四海关，代替市舶司管理对外贸易及征收关税。

公元1686年　专门经营对外贸易的广东十三行成立。

公元1715年　英国在广州设立商馆。

公元1724年　清政府规定前往广州的西方商船一律停泊于黄埔港。

公元1743年　瑞典商船哥德堡号第三次来广州贸易。

公元1757年　清廷关闭江、浙、闽三个海关，仅保留粤海关对外通商，广州成为全国唯一的通商口岸。

公元1784年　美国商船"中国皇后号"首航广州，是为中美两国贸易的开端。

公元1805年　俄国商船首次来广州。

公元1819年　广州至大洋洲的航线开通。

Major Events on the Maritime History of Guangzhou

110B.C. ~ 87B.C.   Emperor Wu sent envoys from Guangdong to countries as far off as Sri Lanka.

A.D.2   The Kingdom of Kanchi (in India nowadays) presented rhinoceros to China by sea.

A.D.166   The Roman Empire sent envoys to China by sea and presented to the Han Emperor the tributes of elephant tusks and rhinoceros horns via Guangdong.

A.D.231   Sun Quan sent Zhu Ying and Kang Tai as envoys to countries in the South China Sea.

A.D.281   The Roman Empire sent delegation to Luoyang via Guangzhou.

A.D.397 ~ 401   The Indian monk Dharmayasas reached Guangzhou and set up a Mahavira Hall inside the Guangxiao Temple.

A.D.412   The Chinese monk Faxian returned from India to Shandong via Guangzhou.

A.D.527   The Indian monk Bodhiharma came to Guangzhou by sea and established there the Xilai'an. The spot where he landed came to be called xilai chudi, literally the first touching of land on journey from the west.

7century   Guangzhou becomes an in portant foreign trade centre. Islamic religion was introduced into China via Guangzhou by sea.

A.D.661   A shiboshi yuan (the office of the Imperial Commissioner of Customs) was set up in Guangzhou to put diplomatic relations and overseas trade under the control of the central government.

A.D.671   The Chinese monk Yijing boarded the Persian boat and left Guangzhou for Bengal to acquire the Buddhist doctrines.

8century   The Arabs built the earliest Islamic place of worship in Guangzhou, namely Huaisheng Mosque, after the religion was spread into China.

A.D.747 ~ 749   The court designated an area in Guangzhou as foreign quarters for the accommodation of Arab and Persian merchants.

A.D.785 ~ 804   The Premier Jia Dan recorded the "Sea Route to Foreign Lands" from Guangzhou to the Persian Gulf.

A.D.971   The Song armies took over the Guangzhou city from the state of Southern Han and set up an in stitution name Shibosi to supervise the overseas trade.

A.D.982   Merchant ships from the Philippines set sail to Guangzhou, opening the maritime trade routes between the two places.

A.D.1071   Envoys from Zanzibar reached Guangzhou by sea, testifying that the maritime trade routes of Song China already extended to East Africa.

A.D.1080   The Song court promulgated the first ordinance in Chinese history to regulate the foreign trade in Guangzhou.

A.D.1286   The Yuan government installed a shibosi in Guangzhou.

A.D.1405   The Ming court set up shibosi in Zhejiang, Fujian and Guangdong provinces, but private trading was still prohibited, a complex of Huaiyuanyi was built in the present-day Shibapu of Guangzhou to accommodate envoys and merchants from various countries.

A.D.1509　Foreign boats from Thailand drifted to Guangdong, whose officials levied commodity taxes and formalized a taxation system on foreign imports.

A.D.1522　Under the threats of the Japanese pirates, the Ming court abolished the two shibosi in Zhejiang and Fujian, merely leaving the one in Guangdong in operation.

A.D.1555 ~ 1566　With Macao as its doorway, the Portuguese established a network of trade routes linking Guangzhou-Macao-Goa-Lisbon at a length of 11,890 nautical miles.

A.D.1583　The Italian Jesuit Matteo Ricci left Macao for Zhaoqing in Guangdong to spread the Gospel.

A.D.1685　Customs offices were set up in Guangzhou, Songjiang, Ningbo and Xiamen, with the dual purpose of managing foreign trade affairs and collecting customs duty.

A.D.1686　The Qing government established the "thirteen hongs" to take charge of the import and export in Guangdong.

A.D.1715　The English Factory was set up in Guangzhou.

A.D.1724　The Qing court ordered that all incoming vessels to Guangzhou anchor at Huangpu.

A.D.1744　The Swedish clipper Gotheborg successfully arrived in Guangzhou the third time.

A.D.1757　The customs offices in Songjiang, Ningbo and Xiamen were closed, leaving Guangzhou as the only port open to foreign trade.

A.D.1784　The American vessel Empress of China landed in Guangzhou, establishing the direct trade between China and the United States.

A.D.1805　The first Russian vessel arrived in Guangzhou.

A.D.1819　The tea clipper Marguis of Hasting departed from Guangzhou to Port Jackson in New South Wales, opening the maritime routes between Guangzhou and the Oceania.

▊后 记▊

　　广州博物馆1929年创建伊始，即以"供专门学者之研究，养成学生事物之观察，奋兴人民文化进展之感想"等为办馆宗旨，以"美术、历史博物、自然科学"为陈列业务发展范围，这在当时是走在全国前列的。正当博物馆事业逐渐走向正轨之际，日本侵略者悍然发动侵华战争，广州沦陷，馆址镇海楼损毁严重，馆藏文物遗失殆尽。抗战胜利后，博物馆又一次提出以地方人文、地方产业、美术、自然科学为陈列业务发展方向，然限于各种原因未能实施。中华人民共和国成立后，博物馆得以恢复并健康发展，到1959年，为庆祝中华人民共和国建国十周年，本馆组织了以广州城市历史为主题的"广州历史陈列"，从而奠定了本馆主体陈列的基础，成为当时全国最早以地方历史为主题展示的地方博物馆之一。遗憾的是，自1966年起，该展览停展达12年之久，至1978年元旦方得复展。此后，该陈列先后进行了多次调整、修改、更新、充实，突显地方特色，深受国内外观众欢迎；到2006年底至2007年初，本馆再次进行了调整，充实展览物品，吸收研究成果，革新展览手法，整合融汇，分十个单元，浓缩了广州六千年的发展历程，展示了广州是岭南文化中心地、海上丝绸之路发祥地、中国民主革命策源地和改革开放前沿地四大特点。在此基础上，本馆同仁群策群力，将该展览编辑成册，具体分工如下：文物图片由本馆文物保护管理部提供；文字编辑由陈列研究部负责，其中"文明曙光"、"南越国都"、"岭南都会"、"广州得名"由黄庆昌、陈鸿钧编辑，"天子南库"、"南汉国都"、"三城合一"由曾玲玲编辑，"帝国商行"、"得风气之先"由王成兰编辑，"英雄城市"由李民涌编辑，英文翻译的校对由教育推广部邓玉梅、周全斌负责，全书由程存洁负责编审。广州市文物考古研究所、南越王宫博物馆筹建处、增城博物馆、西汉南越王博物馆为本书提供了部分文物图片，在此敬表谢意！

　　广州历史悠久，内容丰富，诚非本图册所能囊括，挂一漏万，在所难免，敬祈方家批评指教。

　　　　　　　　　　　　　　　　　　　　　　　　　　《广州历史陈列图册》编委会

封面设计　梁丽辉
责任编辑　程同根
责任印制　张　丽

图书在版编目（ＣＩＰ）数据

广州历史陈列图册／广州博物馆编. —北京：
文物出版社，2009.5
ISBN 978-7-5010-2770-5

Ⅰ.广… Ⅱ.广… Ⅲ.文物—广州市—图集
Ⅳ.K873.65

中国版本图书馆CIP数据核字（2009）第065782号

广 州 历 史 陈 列 图 册

广州博物馆　编

＊

文 物 出 版 社 出 版 发 行

（北京市东直门内北小街2号楼）

http:// www.wenwu.com
E-mail:web@wenwu.com

广 州 伟 龙 印 刷 制 版 有 限 公 司

新 华 书 店 经 销

889×1194　　1/16　印张：21

2009年5月第1版　2009年5月第1次印刷

ISBN 978-7-5010-2770-5　定价：288.00元